# YOUR BALANCING ACT

## DISCOVERING NEW LIFE THROUGH
## FIVE DIMENSIONS OF WELLNESS

*by*

Carolyn J. Taylor M.N.C.S.

*Published by*

## METAMORPHOUS PRESS
P.O. Box 10616
Portland, Oregon 97210-0616

Taylor, Carolyn J.
    Your balancing act.

    Bibliography: p.
    1. Medicine and psychology.    2. Holistic medicine.
I. Title.
R726.5.T38  1985        613        85-31516
ISBN 0-943920-75-2  (pbk.)

Typography by Cy-Ann Designs, Portland, Oregon

Printed in U.S.A.

# DEDICATION

This book is dedicated to my family: my husband, Chet, and my children, Robert, Jill, and James who have helped me develop this model as we lived through the process in the quest of human excellence and wholeness.

# ACKNOWLEDGEMENT

I wish to express my gratitude to John Grinder who encouraged the writing and fine tuning of this wellness model through the example of pursuing human excellence. I would like to express equal appreciation to Richard Bandler, Robert Dilts, and Leslie Cameron-Bandler, and a whole team of trainers in the various NLP certification programs whose capacity to risk with courage and tenacity shared this powerful new technology with a larger group of people.

My thanks to my parents, Robert and Mildred Jones, who gave me the endurance and faith to follow my own star.

A special thanks to my husband, Chet, whose love, forbearance and support cultivated my originality in living and building this model.

My gratitude, love, and respect goes to my daughter Jill, who through her own struggles for wholeness, has affected and stimulated the development and organization of the model.

To my son James, special appreciation for his love and caring, along with his business and "computer genius" which gave me the technology to accomplish the task.

To my son Robert and wife Julie, an expression of thanks for their support and love in encouraging the living of wholeness.

Last but not least, thanks to my very first client and friend, Margaret Louise Hunt, for her editing and writing skills, as well as her loyalty, devotion and display of growth.

# TABLE OF CONTENTS

# PURPOSE

The purpose of this book is to assist others to become "whole."
I believe in health and optimum wellness on all levels in individuals,
families, communities, and in the world. It is my desire to assist individuals to discover not only what is preventing balance, and internal conflicts in their lives, but also to discover what resources are
available for their own restoration. I want to help people discover
their own clues to increased success. The successbook presents
methods that give people more choices in life if they accept responsibility for themselves and are willing to take charge of their own
lives. Self discovery is exciting and creates electricity for us. It is
my hope that by beginning with the individual, higher levels of wellness can spread world wide.

# INTRODUCTION

The following book will be your guide on an adventure into your own capacity for wholeness. Pick a quiet spot for yourself away from distractions and take colored pencils and a pen or pencil with you. Begin by reading Pearl's Great Price and continue reading until you complete the chapter on Optimum Wellness. Be relaxed and trust your subconscious to guide you. Follow the instructions step by step and you will know how much of the exercises to complete at one sitting. In each chapter there is a process to clear a space, to focus, and to integrate information available to you. Out of that process, you will assess, implement a plan and create steps for action toward a desired state of health.

# PEARL'S GREAT PRICE

Once upon a time a beautiful Princess named Pearl, who was full of gladness, cheerfulness and illumination, lived in a castle in the very center of a magic village, called Centralia, which radiated light, warmth and peace. The people in this village were kind, generous and courteous toward each other. There were few unfavorable influences and almost everyone prospered, living in optimum health.

One day when Pearl was walking through the village, she noticed to the left of the village, a dense forest. She rushed home to tell her parents (the King and Queen) of her discovery. She was told never to venture into the forest, for it was an unsafe place to be, full of evil, pain, and suffering. Her parents were trying to protect her.

However, Princess Pearl felt self-reliant, full of curiosity, and she had a desire for adventure. She skipped through the village and thought: "It couldn't be as bad as my father is telling me, and I want to experience some of this for myself." Her adventurous spirit prevailed and she decided to take a walk into the forest. She climbed over the wall surrounding the little magic village and immediately found herself in the very dense forest.

At first, it was very exciting as she crawled through thicket and brushed aside branches, for she saw strange things she had never seen before, as she had always lived in a positive, clean, safe and happy environment.

All at once, however, she realized that it was becoming darker and that a mist was falling all around her. Pearl became very frightened. She found herself hopelessly lost in the midst of the darkness. The more she walked into the forest, the deeper and thicker became the darkness and mist. She could see no light, nor landmarks that would assist her. She fell to the ground, cried hysterically, and screamed for help.

Suddenly, she felt a sharp object pressed against her chest. She looked up and saw a Black Knight, who held a shining sword. His rough voice had a horrifying sound. Having never been exposed to this kind of treatment before, Pearl became even more bewildered and frightened. The people in her village had always treated each other respectfully, with a deep sense of adoration and consideration. It was horrifying for her to be in this situation.

The Black Knight snatched her up from the ground and carried her off into the darkness on his horse. After riding for what seemed to be hours, they finally arrived at a huge castle which was totally different from her own. Everyone at this castle wore black hoods covering their faces. She was brought into a large throne room and interrogated. She was asked what she was doing in the forest, and when she explained, she was rebuked severely, ridiculed and laughed at. She was told that she had entered into forbidden territory and therefore, would have to be punished. She was astounded, since she had never been treated that way before.

Princess Pearl was thrown into a dark dungeon where she spent the night defenseless and frightened. She cried herself to sleep on the cold hard stone floor.

The next day the Dark Knight questioned Pearl at length and discovered that she came from the Village of Love and Caring. The knight was extremely angry, for he knew of the village, Centralia, and he and his people had been trying unsuccessfully to conquer it for many, many years.

The princess was placed in chains and bondage. How she wished she had listened to what her father had told her about the forest. She wished she had not been so adventuresome, since the realization was coming to her that she might die before seeing her father again.

The dark knight decided the princess would become a servant at the castle and he let her out of the chains. She was forced to work as a scullery maid. She was given very little nourishment, and was beaten when she asked questions. Her life was gloomy. She was aware that there was no way to escape from the castle without help. She felt she had no friends, and was isolated and alone in this dark world. "I do wish my father would help me out of this dilemma," she exclaimed!

Then, one day when she was washing out huge black pots she sensed a presence around her. Suddenly, she felt a tap on her shoulder. She turned around and discovered a little green Elf with pointed shoes and hat. At first, she was frightened and thought he might do her harm, but the Elf said, "My name is Guidan, and I can help you, if you wish." "How can you help me?" the princess asked. "If you will listen to what I have to say and follow me, you can leave this castle and return home. I have magic powers that will assist you. But in order to leave this castle, you must do exactly as I tell you. I have discovered an underground tunnel below the forest which leads into your own village. I am the only one who knows of its existence, and how to reach it, and so you will have to trust me."

"Who are you?" asked Princess Pearl.

I am a Wizard called Guidan. I was sent to this area to assist people to make the transition from this "Dark Place," back into the light. I masquerade as an elf who plays the court jester. Nobody pays any attention to me and what I am doing, since people believe I am innocuous. It is a very difficult journey from one spot to another, but very rewarding. You only can travel underground through the castle at a very specific time. I have to watch very carefully, because if I am ever discovered, I will be killed. My death would prevent other people from leaving this dark place and reaching the light.

I have helped many other people, and I know that I will be able to assist you. I want to be your friend. Be prepared to leave at a moment's notice. There will be only one chance, and it will be when you least expect it. Be ready to move at that time. I will contact you. Remember it will be a perilous journey, but an extremely rewarding one. Alligators, poisonous snakes, spiders, man eating fish, and tigers will try to kill you because they do not want anyone to escape from the "Dark Place" into the "Light". But, if you will follow me, you will be safe, because I will give you what is necessary and help you bring yourself out of the "Dark Place" into the "Light".

Princess Pearl was very thrilled and felt very happy about the opportunity to return to her loved ones. But after Guidan left, the days, weeks, and months dragged on very slowly. Pearl thought that Guidan was possibly only a figment of her imagination, that in fact, she had dreamed the whole encounter with him. She became saddened and disheartened as she was forced to cook, scrub, clean, weave, and spin a gold tapestry. She was commanded to do things no one else wanted to do, and if she did not work fast enough, she was beaten. The spinning of the gold tapestry had to be done late at night. If she was found sleeping, she was beaten. She was not given enough food to keep her strong and healthy, and when she became weak and unable to produce, she was cursed and beaten even more severely. This was a most frightening experience for the princess. Finally, as a result of the whole experience, she became gravely ill. She was totally alone without support or help.

One day she was lying on the cot in her grubby little room, half delirious and almost certain she was dying, when she saw Guidan again. She did not believe her eyes; she felt that she was hallucinating. Guidan told Pearl that now was the time for her to leave the horrible Dark Place. She said, "I am too weak and sick to leave. I have no more energy left." Guidan said, "I have magic potions that give strength and energy." She took the magic herbs and they immediately cleared her head.

Then Guidan brought the Princess a Golden cape which he said was magical and was to be worn during the entire journey because it would be her safety and security. He also brought her a silver wand with a brilliant diamond five-pointed star on the end, which illuminated a purple and white hue. Guidan told her it would prevent her from being attacked as she went through the dark cave and tunnel.

At this time the entire castle was asleep. Guidan and Princess Pearl stole down through the castle to the dungeon area. In this area was a small waterway or channel leading away from the dark castle. Guidan assisted her into a little boat, and they moved very, very quietly underneath the castle. It was imperative that they go at this time because the giant alligators were less likely to attack. Pearl was extremely frightened and yet, felt secure with the Wizard, since she trusted him and realized he was her only hope of returning to her homeland. She also remembered her silver wand with the diamond star would cause danger to disappear. She turned around to thank Guidan and discovered he was gone.

So, she continued further down the channel in the boat. She floated to a platform to tie up the boat. As she climbed onto it, Pearl discovered a huge green snake. Pearl was so startled and frightened, she screamed. This awakened and alerted the snake of her presence. In her fear she dropped the silver wand in front of the snake, who was now coiled and in an attack position. She was totally immobilized. However, suddenly she remembered that Guidan, the Wizard, had told her one of the gift's that would protect her was her "Golden Magic Cape." She pulled it tightly around her, and the snake relaxed and lost interest in attacking. She had discovered this was truly a cape of invisibility; therefore, she was able to reach down and pick up her silver wand and tap the snake with it. She was immediately freed of his threat and he disintegrated.

She returned to the boat and continued softly through the channel. Then as she veered along side the wall, the boat struck it and awakened an alligator. This alligator had a blue glistening skin which had a mesmerizing affect on people and made its attack easy. But it was startled, and therefore, attacked before Pearl was totally immobilized. Pearl knew her only hope was to touch the alligator with her magic silver wand. Just in the knick of time she raised her silver wand and touched the alligator on the head. It immediately disintegrated!

Pearl was now feeling very happy about having overcome two dangerous encounters. As she floated on down the channel, she suddenly reached the end and realized she would now have to walk through a tunnel in the dark. She came upon a wall, and looked up and saw a huge yellow spider weaving a web across her path. She pulled out her silver wand and touched it with the diamond star. She was instantly freed, for the spider and its web disintegrated.

She walked for what seemed like hours. In some parts of the tunnel she had to crawl on her hands and knees. There seemed only to be enough light to see a short distance. Then she arrived in a larger area with a high wall, and crouched in a corner sleeping was a large orange tiger. Fortunately, she saw him before he awakened. When he saw her, he made one ferocious growl and leaped toward her. This time she was ready with the "Golden Cape" wrapped around her and easily touched the center of his head with the diamond star from the silver Wand. The tiger disintegrated as easily as the others.

With each battle she overcame, her internal strength and confidence grew. At the end of the tunnel, Pearl came upon another large body of water and there on the edge waiting was Guidan, the Wizard. She was so happy to see him. He told her this was the last and most treacherous part of the journey. She would have to climb onto a raft, cross the water to the other side of the cave, because there was no bridge. He told her to be very careful and have the silver wand ready because a crafty, evil being, called Gruell that was part man and part fish lived in the water. She climbed onto the raft and prepared to cross the narrow waterway, but suddenly, the water rippled, and the nasty, evil looking Gruell appeared. He swam very close to the raft, but she was prepared, and touched his body with the diamond star. A huge burst of purple light filled the entire area and Gruell disintegrated, and what swam off in its place was a beautiful white fish that said, "Thank you Princess for freeing me, I will be eternally grateful."

Princess Pearl arrived across the water to the farthest end of the cave, to complete the last lap of the journey. She began to notice a freer and happier feeling within her than she'd ever experienced before. She kept walking uphill, but soon discovered that the passageway was becoming narrower and narrower to the point where she had to crawl on her hands and knees again, but she was being motivated on by a brilliant light ahead. She crawled out of a small opening and drew herself up by grasping a small bush located just outside. Soon, she had pulled her whole body out. The light was so bright it hurt her eyes, but she realized immediately that she was back outside the wall of her own beautiful, happy little Magic Village.

Pearl continued on until she found a spot where she could climb a tree and reach the top of the wall. It was a difficult tree to climb, with many long, sharp thorns; however, she kept right on climbing though she pricked both of her hands so that they were bleeding badly. She was afraid she would lose so much blood that it would not be possible to continue; however, her second wind revived her and she was determined. Finally she could jump down on the wall.

As Pearl landed on the wall, her silver wand slipped and fell. When it struck the ground with a flash, it turned into a beautiful white Unicorn. She straddled his back and was carried over the wall and landed in the very center of the Magic Village. The people recognized Princess Pearl at once, even though she was tattered, torn, dirty, and bleeding. At this point, the Unicorn changed into a Handsome Prince. The Princess's father and mother (King and Queen), came out to greet her and embraced and welcomed her home. Her parents said, "We thought you were lost and would never be found. We are so happy you have returned." She was immersed in a healing pool, that healed her wounds immediately. She was then clothed in beautiful silver and gold garments.

Much joy and happiness radiated throughout the Village as their Princess told of her travels and particularly her last, most perilous journey. As a result of this whole experience, Princess Pearl was able to bring news to the Magic Village about the Dark Place and how she had been able to return to the Channel of Life with the help of Guidan the Wizard. Everyone noticed the confidence and maturity the Princess now exuded. Not only did she possess loveliness and compassion, but her outer beauty was matched by her inner beauty and inner strength that no one could take from her. So, this was a wonderful, beautiful day, in which Princess Pearl married her Handsome Prince. And she lived a very long, happy, creative and fruitful life.

# DISCOVERY

The seed of the wellness model sprouted over thirty years ago when I was a young eighteen year old student nurse. I was educated to the belief like the rest of the medical community, that someone "outside myself" would tell me what was wrong and what needed to be done about health. Serious doubts about this process arose when I recognized that the medical model was only able to deal with the symptoms of my patients. Patients were not cured; the symptoms just subsided. We never seemed to be able to find the root cause of many illnesses, and it seemed like there were many re-admissions for the same disease process. I watched patients and close friends die with incurable diseases and felt frustrated and helpless. This prompted me to search for my own answers to wellness. As the seedling grew, my curiosity was overwhelming. It was challenging and exciting at the same time. I would come to a spot in a newly discovered process and think I had discovered the whole solution, only to stumble across another missing piece to the puzzle, which led me to realize that there were many disciplines in the health field that held a piece to the whole. This budding exploration eventually centered on five dimensions of life: physical, social, mental, emotional, and spiritual. As human beings, most of our life's processes can be listed in one of the five areas. I have discovered that for me to feel optimum wellness and to prevent dis-ease, I need to maintain a balance in these five life areas. My presupposition was it would also be true for others. I began testing this out with patients, students, family, and friends who also believed that it was true for them. Later, as a nurse practitioner, I developed a private counseling practice and began using the principles with clients and discovered it had a lasting effect with them also. I was aware that when we are younger, there is more tolerance for imbalance in these five areas than there is with added maturity. Over time, with added imbalances, the body begins to break down and physical debilitation is more prevalent. This process of balancing the five areas of life allows me to take responsibility for my own health, acknowledge my own power, learn to trust my own "inside" answers, and give the same freedom to those I work with.

My search for wellness blossomed as I read, listened to others' inner wisdom as well as my own, and experienced confidence in my own growth and change. My seeking has been long, and is not over, for it will continue as long as I live on this earth. In some respects I feel like I am just beginning as is best expressed in C. S. Lewis's *Chronicles of Narnia, The Last Battle*:

"But for them it was only the beginning of the real story. All their life in this world and all their adventures in Narnia had only been the cover and the title page: now at last they were beginning Chapter One of the Great Story, which no one on earth has read: which goes on forever; in which every chapter is better than the one before."

I believe integrated wellness comes when we experience balance and integration of the physical, social, emotional, mental, and spiritual dimensions of life. A good example of this model of wholeness in the body is the hands.

Can you imagine what it would be like if each finger decided to do something different from the other? Chaos and confusion would reign and nothing would be accomplished until some agreement could be made between all fingers.

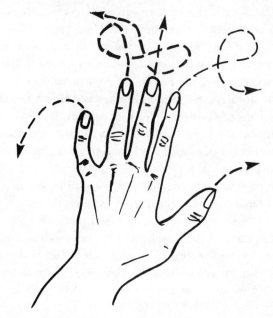

Or, can you imagine what it would be like for one finger to be grossly larger or smaller than the other?

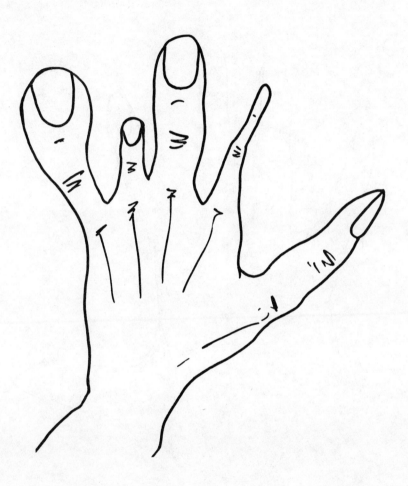

Be aware that the body would compensate, but do you have a sense of the energy it would take for a hand to function in this state. We allow this to happen in our bodies by being out of balance and out of harmony with the universe.

Now be aware of the hand in balance, fingers working together. Notice the difference, and how much more functional and freer the hand is in this state. "The Whole is Greater than the Sum of its parts."

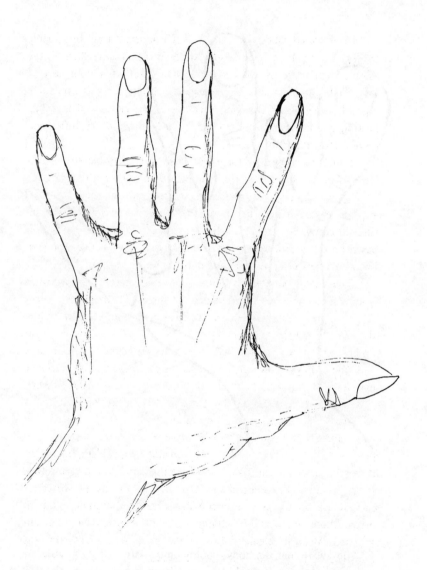

# CHAPTER ONE

# GO FOR HEALTH

I discovered modern medicine is a wonderful tool, but people expect too much of it and too little of themselves. Wellness is the right and privilege of every person. No matter what your current state of health is at this moment, you can imagine and appreciate yourself as a growing, changing, precious individual, as well as seeing, hearing, and feeling yourself moved towards a happier, healthier, and more joyful, abundant life.

Taking responsibility for maintaining your own health involves changes in the way the world is perceived and our attitudes toward it. The average person has grown up refusing to take responsibility and has passed it over to the doctor, Medicare, or some health insurance company. The result has been a creation of a relationship based on dependency rather than one based on a creative, cooperative effort between physician and patient.

Back in the Nineteenth Century, Louis Pasteur developed what is known today as the "germ theory of disease." The consequences of the germ theory is germs cause disease, and they must be destroyed. Therefore, the emphasis in medicine has been placed on finding drugs to kill germs. There have been some very positive results with some drugs. However, in the process, we have almost become a nation that believes in the "Pill Fairy" according to John Travis, M.D.

A French scientist by the name of Claude Bernard (1927), a colleague of Pasteur had a different view of the same problem. He was a physiologist (unlike Pasteur, who was a bacteriologist) who proposed that the germ or bacteria was not the problem, but rather it was the internal environment in which the germs found themselves. If the internal environment was fertile for germs, disease would result. If the body was in proper balance and functioning in equilibrium, the germs would be eliminated and the system would be untouched. Medical science followed the germ theory. Pasteur was quoted as saying on his death bed, however: "Bernard was right. It is not the germ, but the internal milieu."

It is believed by many researchers and physicians that the most single contradiction to the germ theory of disease is the so-called "placebo" effect. Sugar pills given in the place of real medication (without the patient's knowledge) continues to produce remarkable symptom relief in a large number of patients. Dr. Elliott M. Goldwag in the book *Inner Balance* reports: "In one reported study in 1956, it was found that of 1,000 patients treated, 35.2% obtained satisfactory relief from the symptoms studied by being given an innocuous pill. The symptoms included severe postoperative wound pain, the pain of angina pectoris, headache, cough, mood change, seasickness, anxiety, and the common cold (Beecher 1956). In another more recent study, Haas, Fink, and Hartfelder (1963) reported that out of 14,177 patients with various ills, 40.6% obtained relief from the placebo (sugar pills). This means that patients who thought they were given medication for their problem actually received a sugar pill. "Dr. Jerome Frank (1973) formerly chairman of the Department of Psychiatry at John Hopkins University medical school called the "faith" effect, which is the patient's believing in the physician or the drug helping him feel better is another demonstration of the "placebo" effect. The theory is that if the patient's belief is strong enough in the doctor and what is suggested, it will relieve symptoms, and the relief will last as long as the strength of the belief is maintained. Also, in a study done with patients having experienced healing in cancer, it was discovered the single ingredient expressed as most important to the process was, belief that whatever treatment being administered would work. Walter B. Cannon, a well-known physiologist and physician who taught at Harvard Medical School for many years, developed the now universally accepted concept of "homeostasis" in his book *The Wisdom of The body* (1939). Cannon in 1926 proposed that the body which is composed of unstable material and is subjected to continuous disturbing conditions has internal regulators always attempting to maintain a constant state of equilibrium. When a factor is known to shift a homeostatic situation in one direction, other factors will pull in another direction. It is like we have regulators that maintain our internal environment so that these fluctuations occur in narrow limits in response to internal and external environment. Many processes happen simultaneously, providing continuous feedback in order to maintain balance. Each person is unique and responds to stimulus differently. For example: in some individuals exercise stimulates thyroid function, while in others it has the opposite effect. Apparently both Cannon and Bernard subscribed to the value of all forces in the body working in an intimate relationship to keep all of them functioning within very narrow limits of disruption in order to maintain equilibrium and a positive internal environment. They both saw the biological function as an integrated whole and each part dependent on the other for synchronists, which required no conscious effort on the body's part to maintain coordination and automatic functioning.

Sigmund Freud (1943) known as the father of psychiatry who originally was a neurophysiologist, introduced his theory of the unconscious influence being responsible for behavior and for certain types of illness. Freud believed an internal set of forces of the mind distinct from the body known as the brain called id, ego, and superego, are forces formed in early years of childhood. He further believed these programmed patterns of behavior are responding to meet the needs of unconscious drives. Therefore, Freud's theory supported Claude Bernard's biological explanation of the internal environment and brought forth what we might call today a unitary concept of disease.

## Unified Medicine Means:

A. A need to study the pathogens and their effects on people as well as people who are affecting the behavior of pathogens.

B. Man is more than just a body. He is a mind that thinks and influences biochemical and physiologic functions.

C. Man is related to all other living things in the universe, and has a purpose beyond surviving.

D. Man is a part of a higher, cosmic spiritual force.

E. Being more interested in the lifestyle rather than the laboratory report.

F. Spending time to discover stressors in a person's life that may - indicate a belief system that may be damaging and cause dis-e ease and imbalance.

G. The individual is seen as a functioning person rather than a condition.

H. Co-operating with the right-brain intuitive sense (a kind of "tuning in") to discover what's really going on or be aware of what the body is experiencing.

I. Accepting that germs are agents of disease, but recognizing stress is the real basis of illness, since stress is the response chosen consciously or unconsciously to adapt to internal or external threats.

J.    Believing that perception of the world is an individual matter and varies from one person to another.

Dr. Hans Selye made one of the greatest single contributions to world medicine and to our understanding of causes of disease. He concentrated on intuitive insights, and careful observations of people, which led to the development of the theory of stress as a basis for illness. More and more we are becoming aware in a greater degree how stress effects our lives. For example: ulcers, asthma, glaucoma, hypertension, cardiovascular problems, diabetes, cancer, arthritis, rheumatism and allergies are but a few stress related illnesses.

Freedom rests within each individual to choose the way he or she perceives the world internally and externally. It is no longer possible to be fooled into thinking that outside forces control our destiny. It is important to assume the responsibility that the power which created disharmony and disequilibrium is a force that is invented by ourselves and can be used to create harmony and balance. This power is like electricity that goes where it is directed to go. When we are able to assist people to look at certain important beliefs about themselves, then we are coming to the basic cause of illness, and may help to change the course of individual and societal wellness consciousness. Albert Einstein has summed up these principles when he said:

"A human being is a part of the whole, called by us "universe," a part limited in time and space. He experiences himself, his thoughts and feelings, as something separate from the rest — a kind of optical delusion of his consciousness. This delusion is a kind of prison for us, restricting us to our personal decisions and to affection for a few persons nearest to us. Our task must be to free ourselves from this prison by widening our circle of compassion to embrace all living creatures and the whole nature in its beauty."

It is out of these premises that I have developed over my lifetime the model of wholeness presented in the following pages. The key for me was accepting responsibility for my own wellness.

Self responsibility for wellness was a turning point for my positive health. To me it means:

1. Discovering personal needs and meeting them with many

choices which are appropriate, in my own way, and in my own time.

2. Tuning in to inner wisdom and recognizing, "what the body is saying".

3. Seeing, feeling, and hearing the uniqueness and expertness of self.

4. Creating appropriate choices really wanted rather than re-acting to situations in life.

5. Being able to enjoy the body through food, exercise and physical awareness.

6. Expressing emotions appropriately to communicate to other people what is being experienced assertively.

7. Cultivating and developing close relationships with new and old friends.

8. Being involved in projects and experiences that are meaning-ful and purposeful.

Milton H. Erickson, M.D., who died in March 1980, was prob-ably the most dynamic and creative hypnotherapist the world has ever known. As a psychotherapist he was genuinely impressed by how much people knew but did not know that they knew. He be-lieved some of this knowledge consisted of psychological, emotional, physical, or intellectual information that originally was consciously acquired but dropped out of conscious awareness. He believed people could learn without consciously knowing that they had learned and could use these learnings later without recognizing that they were doing so. It is believed this type of learning occurs since the unconscious is a separate parallel system of awareness and in-formation processing. Although a large part of behavior is uncon-scious or automatic, most of what we do intentionally or consciously is dependent upon the use of unconsciously held learnings. Also, a large part of what we have learned and know is not applied or used effectively by us due to our conscious repressions and inflexibility. This is best summed up by a statement made by Milton Erickson when he said, "Your unconscious does know much more about you than you do. It's got a whole background of years of learning, feel-ing, thinking, and doing. And all our days we are learning things — learning how. Human beings, once they have learned anything, transfer this learning to the forces that govern their bodies." (In Erickson, 1980. Vol. III, chapter 4 p. 27) Dr. Erickson respected the wisdom of the body, and constantly referred to the creativity held inside of each person.

The following quote from a taped lecture of Dr. Erickson's on July 16, 1965, describes the discovery process which works for me as I learned to trust the process:

"Because the important understanding that you need is this, that any knowledge acquired by your unconscious mind is knowledge that you can use at any appropriate time. But you need not necessarily be aware that you have the knowledge until the moment comes to use it. And then you just quite naturally respond with the appropriate behavior."

This trusting of one's self for answers is both exciting and rewarding as creativity and self-confidence is increased. This is supported by a man called Galileo back in the 15th century when he stated:

*"You cannot teach a man anything, you can only help him discover it down inside himself."*

I believe this statement is true for each individual as it has been for me. Therefore, this text is set up for each person to discover wellness for themselves. So, let's begin by discovering what wellness is for you. You are a unique individual, and it is important this be your own discovery, since permanent changes happen in this way.

# CHAPTER TWO

# INTEGRATED MODEL OF WELLNESS

## DESCRIPTION

Wellness can be a way of life now. You can choose to enjoy life to the fullest. As human beings, we have an innate desire to change, grow and be fulfilled. This "something" within each of us has been called the "growth principle." It throbs in every cell and actually vibrates in the pulsating atoms, neutrons and electrons which comprise each cell. It is referred to as the force which prompts the cell to divide, or the child to grow. It is responsible for ambition, aspiration, reverence, and awe. As you aspire to be more than you are, love more, and grow more, you become more motivated to be whole and fulfilled. This is the Life Force at work within you. Wellness is not just absence of dis-ease, it is optimum performance and personal success in all aspects of our lives. It is freedom to concentrate your energies in positive, uplifting endeavors. We believe this can happen for all people if they so choose. It is a personal decision as well as a personal responsibility. No one does wellness for or to you. Wellness . . . is personal to each individual; and therefore, must be defined individually. It is a quality, a standard of mind and body. Your beliefs about health and wellness will set the standard for yourself and your life now and in the days to come.

It is this frame of reference that motivated and inspired me to prepare this successbook, in an effort to assist myself and others to pursue the path of wholeness directly. The successbook has been designed for you to discover and explore wellness beliefs and values, habits, weaknesses, strengths, interferences and blocks by balancing these areas which I have categorized as the five dimensions of life: physical, social, emotional, mental, and spiritual.

I have also included in this model the "nursing process." According to Yura and Walsh in their book entitled *Nursing Process* (1978): The components of the process are: assessment, planning, implementation, and evaluation. I have modified it some by using the self discovery method. This gives the patient more responsibility. The nursing process is used in each dimension as well as the overall picture.

I have been influenced by the general systems theory which was initially proposed by Ludwig von Bertalanffy (1968), as the framework is useful for describing wholeness. The human race is an example of an open system. We interact with the environment by taking information, energy, and material in, processing the information and returning it into the environment in different forms. Each part affects the other parts as well as the whole. When one part changes, another part needs to change to maintain homeostasis. A group of parts makes the whole, and when changes happen, the whole is affected. For example: The famine in Ethiopia has affected the world's attitude towards hunger and helping other people. It resulted in people all over the world raising money to help feed the hungry.

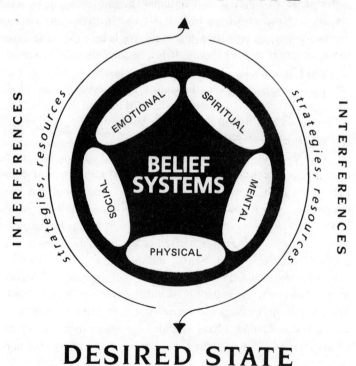

PRESENT STATE

INTERFERENCES    strategies, resources    EMOTIONAL    SPIRITUAL    strategies, resources    INTERFERENCES

SOCIAL    BELIEF SYSTEMS    MENTAL

PHYSICAL

DESIRED STATE

## MODEL OF WELLNESS

The model of wellness is a process that allows you to discover the balance of your health. The techniques used allow each person to ASSESS, PLAN, IMPLEMENT, and EVALUATE each of the five dimensions.

1. First, ASSESS your present state of health in each of the five dimensions.

2. Second, decide on a realistic desired state of health and formulate a PLAN based on a set of questions that will help you achieve a successful outcome.

3. Third, discover and discard the fears and limitations that have prevented you from having the desired state of health.

4. Fourth, use various techniques, (experiential and cognitive) taken from all sensory systems that will enable you to change from present state of health to the desired state of wellness.

5. Fifth, devise a task to IMPLEMENT the behavior change. Each person's unique strategies and resources will be utilized in this task(s).

6. Sixth, EVALUATE the process through many methods, one of which is called, "future time". This enables the potential flaws or problems to be caught before they happen.

PERSONAL NOTES

# CHAPTER THREE

# DESCRIPTION OF EACH OF FIVE DIMENSIONS

## Physical Dimension

In order to help you assess, plan, implement, and evaluate in the physical dimension, some of the beginning guide lines to consider are suggested here giving you the freedom to enlarge where and when appropriate. Included is everything associated with your body, both internal and external, as well as inputs into the body (such as air, food, and water) and the transformation of these inputs within the body. Outputs from the body such as waste products, energy for exercise, and healing are also a part of this dimension. More specifically, consider the following:

nutrition    breathing    touching    rest    body weight    fitness

genetics    body image    sexuality    environment    energy

circulation    digestion    urinary tract system    immune system

skin/hair    endocrine system

## Social Dimension

In order to assist you to assess, plan, implement, and evaluate in the social dimension, some of the beginning guidelines to consider are suggested here, giving each person the freedom to enlarge when and where appropriate. All of your abilities that enable you to function as a member of society belong in this dimension. Belonging in this area are interactions and relationships with others which are influenced by your physical, social, and cultural environments. You are constantly interacting with society, which brings to the fore front issues of dependence, independence, and interdependence. The self concept is influenced by the way in which we develop degrees of trust and mistrust. The following are more specific areas to consider:

interpersonal skills         family relationsip         peer relationships

verbal communication            non-verbal         socialization (friends)
                              communication

finances

intimacy                     parent issues                 fun and play

beliefs                          values                        customs

attitudes                         goals                        ethnicity

self-esteem                   environment                    community


# Emotional Dimension

The emotional dimension of wellness is the affective or feeling element of awareness. Various theories of emotion attempt to integrate three components:   1) What is expressed.   2) What is felt.   3) What happens inside the body. Motivating yourself to develop more flexible behavior in this dimension is valuable. Feelings may not be seen, heard, or touched, yet they are a very important part of our world. The following are some specific issues included in the emotional dimension and you have the freedom to enlarge the list:

joy        anger        grief        elation        self confidence

aggression        sad        being withdrawn        suspicion        guilt

negativism        being prudish        smugness        ecstasy        hostility

anxiety        fear        jealousy        empathy

## Mental Dimension

The mental dimension is the intellectual area. There are four main categories to consider. According to Lezak in the book *Neuro-physiological Assessment* (1976) they are:  1) Receptivity: the ability to acquire, process, classify, and integrate information.  2) Memory and learning: the means by which memory is stored and recalled.  3) Cognition: mental organization, and reorganization of information.  4) Expression: how information is communicated or acted upon. (p. 14) More specifically the following are included in this dimension:

| | | |
|---|---|---|
| memory | immediate and long term | concentration |
| focusing | concrete    abstract    speaking | drawing |
| writing | flexibility/rigidity | problem solving |
| decision making | acquiring new information | thought control |

## Spiritual Dimension

The spiritual dimension is really the core of an individual's existence, which integrates and transcends the other dimensions. Spirituality has been described as a sensitivity or attachment to religious values. A person's spiritual identity encompasses much more than religious doctrines. It allows us to experience and understand existence beyond our usual limits, and is very different for each individual. To some it is a strong belief in God or a higher power. For others it deals with a purpose in life — why am I here?. When spiritual needs are met satisfactorily, a person is free to function with a meaningful purpose and identity. He/she is able to relate to reality with hope and confidence. Spirituality deals with our philosophy of life. It is best described as a set of standards that guide decision-making about beliefs, values, morals, and ethics. The following are some needs that relate to this dimension:

meaningful philosophy of life      purpose in life      self-actualization

flow with universe                        relatedness to God or higher power

interrelationship of people and nature                        meditation

freedom to choose              faith         awareness of nobler emotions

humanitarianism          ability to let go          living the Golden Rule

transcending ordinary limits                  recognition of others' reality

# CHAPTER FOUR

## OPTIMUM WELLNESS

"Who are you?" asked Princess Pearl.

I am a Wizard called Guidan. I was sent to this area to assist people to make the transition from this "Dark Place," back into the light.....

I have helped many other people, and I know that I will be able to assist you. I want to be your friend. Be prepared to leave at a moment's notice. There will be only one chance, and it will be when you least expect it. Be ready to move at that time. I will contact you. Remember it will be a perilous journey, but an extremely rewarding one. Alligators, poisonous snakes, spiders, man eating fish, and tigers will try to kill you because they do not want anyone to escape from the "Dark Place" into the "Light". But, if you will follow me, you will be safe, because I will give you what is necessary and help you bring yourself out of the "Dark Place" into the "Light".

Close your eyes and go inside. Imagine Jiminey Cricket singing, "Always let your subconscious be your guide." Then allow to come into your awareness a PICTURE THAT BEST REPRESENT TO YOU OPTIMUM WELLNESS. Open your eyes, draw the picture below with colored pencils using whatever colors are appropriate for you.

Looking at a continuum from well to dis-ease — 0 being the sickest, and 10 being optimum wellness, circle the number that best represents your state of wellness right now.

0    1    2    3    4    5    6    7    8    9    10

Now, write a statement about what you desire for yourself in the area of general wellness.

On this page draw a five pointed star and label the points physical, social, emotional, mental, and spiritual. Close your eyes for a moment and imagine in your mind's eye the five pointed star. Notice how each area needs to be colored. Then open your eyes and color the star to represent balance for you in those areas at this moment in time.

## CATHARSIS WRITING

Jiminey Cricket in "Pinocchio" had a favorite little ditty which he sung to Pinocchio, "Always let your conscience be your guide." Imagine Jiminey Cricket singing to you, "Always let your subconsciousness be your guide," as well as your eyes, ears, nose, and mouth. Write OPTIMUM WELLNESS at the top of the next page in your successbook. Set a timer for five minutes. Then begin writing everything that comes to your mind as quickly as possible about your concept, experiences, goals, and fears concerning optimum wellness. Do not stop until the timer rings. (If you have a little difficulty writing the full five minutes, repeat the last sentence you' wrote until a new thought comes into your mind.)

PERSONAL NOTES

Jiminey Cricket in "Pinocchio" had a favorite little ditty which he sung to Pinocchio, "Always let your conscience be your guide." So close your eyes for a moment and imagine him instead singing to you, "Always let your subconscious be your guide," and then say to yourself:

OPTIMUM WELLNESS IS:

Open your eyes and write the first ten words that come to your awareness on this page. You may find yourself being reminded of words as you read a word already written.

1.

2.

3.

4.

5.

6.

7.

8.

9.

10.

Wellness means something different to each person, and each meaning is valid. The following is an example of the exercise you will complete.

## OPTIMUM WELLNESS

| | |
|---|---|
| Abundance | Wellness is an abundance of joy |
| Belonging | which brings belongingness to my soul |
| Prepared | through consistent preparedness. |
| Process | It is a process which allows me a choice in |
| Programming | programming my own health and allows |
| Sharing | me an opportunity for sharing with others. |
| Balancing | It brings balance to my |
| Energetic | energy flow |
| Mobility | which creates and increases mobility |
| Choices | by developing and maintaining new choices. |

Now, connect your words on page 21 in the order you first wrote them to form a sentence or paragraph that makes sense to you. You may add words or change the form of the words you initially wrote to make the connections flow. When you have completed this exercise, you will have discovered what wellness means to you at this time. Thank yourself for the impressive information.

Again, close your eyes and imagine Jiminey Cricket singing "Always let your subconscious be your guide." Say to yourself, "Dis-ease or illness is:" then open your eyes and write the first ten words that come into your awareness.

1.

2.

3.

4.

5.

6.

7.

8.

9.

10.

Connect these words into a sentence or two, or paragraph, using the words in the order listed above. Do this fairly quickly. Again, you have just discovered what dis-ease or illness means to you at this time. Thank yourself for this information.

Close your eyes and go inside yourself and bring back the image of Jiminey Cricket singing "Always let your subconscious be your guide." Then hear yourself saying, "Optimum WELLNESS means to me:" . . . . Then open your eyes and write in the space provided below as quickly as possible the words or phrase that come to your mind. Don't hesitate or analyze the information yet, just write the one or two words that describe best for you the answers to the statement.

## OPTIMUM WELLNESS MEANS:

# CHAPTER FIVE

# USE OF LANGUAGE
## (Predicates)

Predicates are described as process words which could be adjectives, adverbs, or verbs that are used to describe an individual's model of the world. A pattern of preferences for certain predicates becomes evident when a person talks. As you listen to yourself or others talk, you can discover the most frequent use of one system. Bandler and Grinder in early development of NeuroLinguistic Programming suggested that everyone creates a model of the world and that due to neurological, social, and individual constraints, everyone's model of the world is different. It is believed human beings take in information through the five senses: visual, auditory, kinesthetic, olfactory, gustatory. Recently, however, there has been some talk of a sixth sense which has to do with spatial consciousness. Since our sensory organs may vary from person to person, each one perceives the world differently. Carl Jung, a psychiatrist who worked with Sigmund Freud and later developed his own model of dream interpretation, put this process most succinctly when he said in his book, *Man and His Symbols*:

"Man . . . never perceives anything fully or comprehends anything completely. He can see, hear, touch, taste; but how far he sees, how well he hears, what his touch tells him, and what he tastes depend upon the number and quality of his senses . . . No matter what instruments he uses, at some point he reaches the edge of certainty beyond which conscious knowledge cannot pass." (p. 21)

If you pay attention to the language patterns, you can discover what the preferred representational system is for yourself and others. Predicates reveal what part of the experience is most relevant to the speaker at that moment. The theory is, we learn to favor one system over the others. Its use can be believed to be a habit (you're more at home with it) and it is particularly evident during stress, since, we as human beings, return to previously, learned comfortable behavior during stress. Therefore, the system used most often on a conscious and unconscious level to understand our experiences is referred to as the "preferred representational system." The purpose and function with the successbook material is to balance areas of your life, and to do that, you want to be aware of the imbalance. More choices are available as you expand your sensory systems. As you do, you will alter your own behavior as well as that of others. Here are examples of how a person's words reveal his/her representational system and how the situation is being experienced.

## VISUAL

"I SEE what you are saying."
"I LOOK at various approaches."
"What you are saying is not CLEAR."
"Let's get a new PERSPECTIVE."
"You bring BRIGHTNESS into the situation."

## AUDITORY

"TUNE into what is going on."
"LISTEN to what I am saying."
"It SOUNDS like you understand me."
"What you're explaining RINGS a bell for me."
"Suddenly, it all CLICKED in place."

## KINESTHETIC

"I FEEL right about it."
"Can you GRASP what I am saying?"
"Do you have a HANDLE on this?"
"Try to get in TOUCH with what's happening."
"That seems real SOLID."

## GUSTATORY

"That TASTES of trouble."
"She has a SOUR approach to life."
"That is a BITTER pill to SWALLOW."
"His FLAVOR for life is strange."
"That is certainly PALATABLE."

## OLFACTORY

"His ODOR is offensive."
"She REEKS of injustice."
"Can you get the SCENT of the conversation?"
"Did you get a WHIFF of him?"
"The SMELL in here is stagnant."

## REPRESENTATIONAL SYSTEMS

| VISUAL | AUDITORY | KINESTHETIC | OLFACTORY/ GUSTATORY |
|---|---|---|---|
| brightness | hear | feel | taste |
| dim | listen | warm | flavor |
| hazy | talk | touch | savor |
| perspective | harmony | soft | relish |
| focus | loud | rough | pungent |
| view | tone | firm | aftertaste |
| enlighten | amplify | tight | scent |
| perceive | silence | penetrate | with a nose for |
| glimpse | amplify | absorb | leave bad taste in mouth |
| visible | lend an ear | tense | smell |

These are a few. Continue to add to the list.

Predicates which do not indicate any sensory channel are labeled "unspecified." Some examples of these are:

| | | | |
|---|---|---|---|
| think | know | understand | change |
| learn | nice | trusting | respect |
| believe | | remember | consider |

# PERSONAL NOTES

# CHAPTER SIX

## EXPANDING WELLNESS

Return to your optimum wellness list on page 24 and categorize it according to the representational systems described on pages 26 and 27 in order to be aware of more information about yourself and how you are processing optimum wellness information. The purpose is to allow more choices in your life. "In cybernetics there is a principle which is known as the law of requisite variety. The law states that in any connected interacted system, the element that has the widest range of variability in behavior will be, ultimately, the controlling element. NLP Volume 1 (p. 151) Therefore simply stated, "the organism with the most choices ends up on top." Awareness is the first step to change and more flexibility.

## VISUAL                    AUDITORY                    KINESTHETIC

## OLFACTORY / GUSTATORY                 UNSPECIFIED

As you look through this information just completed and become more aware of the process and the thoughts you are having about your own state of health and well being, answer the statements following.

What do you want in relation to optimum wellness?

How will you know when you have optimum wellness for you?

When and where do you want optimum wellness?

What does not having optimum wellness do for you? How does it assist you?

What will having optimum wellness do for you? How would your life change?

What stops you from having optimum wellness?

What resources do you now have to help you move towards your wellness goal?

What resources do you now need to help you take the first step toward your wellness goal?

What would be a demonstration or tangible sign that you have what you want in optimum wellness? How would you know when you had achieved optimum wellness?

Set a task for yourself in relationship to optimum wellness that once it was accomplished, you would know you have achieved your goal. Limit the time period to reach this goal to prove to yourself you're serious about your desire for and are in process with optimum wellness. Write down the time and expected completion date. You will widen your choices if you choose a task in an area where your predicates indicate imbalance. For example:

If you have learned from the exercises so far, that you experience the world primarily through vision (your list of vision words on page 30 is long) set a task for yourself that is kinesthetic or auditory.

a.  A visual person might want to set up more exercise to broaden kinesthetic.

b.  A kinesthetic person who wants to lose weight may want to notice clothes on thin people for a period of time and imagine wearing the outfit themselves to broaden visual external.

c.  An auditory person may want to focus on a person's face and listen to external sounds of words, notice where feelings are located in own body.

## INTERFERENCES/FEAR:    What Stops You From Achieving Optimum Wellness?

Take an 8½ by 11 sheet of paper and divide it into four columns and list across as follows:

Interferences/Fear    Experience Causing It    Intention    Behavior

Close your eyes and go inside, see and hear Jiminey Cricket singing, "Always let your subconscious be your guide," and be aware of your feelings. Then ask yourself, "What stops me from achieving optimum wellness?" Open your eyes and begin writing in Column 1 as quickly as possible the interferences or fear that prevents you from success in the optimum wellness you want.

In Column 2 write the experience you believe causes this fear. You may get a picture of a memory, have a feeling, or hear something being said by yourself or others when you do this. Write it down briefly.

In Column 3 which is labeled Intention write what that interference had done for you in a positive way. (Every behavior has a positive intention, though the results we experience are often negative. Often the intention is self-protection.)

In Column 4 write two or three things you can do to replace the interference with new behaviors that satisfy the intention. (When we have choices in life, most individuals are freer and have a decrease in internal stress.)

For example: New behaviors are: Get counseling, acknowledge to my mate that my emotional needs aren't being met, change the pictures in my head, change the way I talk to myself about it.

| Interference Fear | Cause | Intention | New Behavior |
|---|---|---|---|
|  |  |  |  |

For example: One of my INTERFERENCES to achieving the optimum wellness state I desire might be *over-eating*.

EXPERIENCE CAUSING IT: I remember being given food to comfort me as a child when I felt upset.

INTENTION: Comfort and Satisfaction.

NEW BEHAVIOR CHOICES:
  a.   Relaxation time in a hot tub.
  b.   Going to a funny movie.
  c.   Going window shopping.
  d.   Running.

This is unique to each person — for what is comfort for one is stress for another.

When you are ready to be free of interferences/fears:

1.   Tear off the part labeled interferences/fears — experience causing it and THROW IT IN THE GARBAGE OR BURN IT.
2.   Save the intention and behavior and clip it to your successbook page. Go back to the task set up for yourself as a demonstration of this process, and commit yourself to accomplishing it.

| Interference Fear | Cause | Intention | New Choice Behavior |
|---|---|---|---|
| overeating | food=comfort | comfort satisfaction | 1. Relax in a hot tub<br>2. See a funny movie<br>3. Go window shopping<br>4. Run<br>(These will satisfy the need for comfort or satisfaction) |

Tear Here and Discard

## PERSONAL NOTES

# CHAPTER SEVEN

# DISCOVERING SURFACE BELIEFS
## (Submodalities)

Submodalities, patterns developed by Richard Bandler in the last few years, is a powerful yet simple tool to use by yourself. In Richard Bandlers' new book entitled *Using Your Brain For A Change*, submodalities are explained in this way:

"One of the earliest NLP patterns was the idea of 'Modalities' or 'Representational Systems.' We think about any experience we have using sensory system representations — visual pictures, auditory sounds and kinesthetic feelings. Most NLP training during the last ten years has taught a wide variety of rapid and practical ways to use this knowledge of modalities to change feelings and behavior. Submodalities are the smaller elements within each modality. For example, a few of the visual submodalities are: brightness, color, size, distance, location, and focus. Knowledge of Submodalities opens up a whole new reality of change patterns that are even faster, easier and more specific" (page 2) than traditional therapy.

The following examples from Bandler's submodality work are: Take a pleasant memory from your past and make the colors stronger and more intense. How does this affect the feeling intensity? Now make that picture black and white. How does this affect your state? Most people have a weaker response as the color is lost. Brightness and sparkle are two salient features that have an intense response for most people. Throughout this successbook program submodalities will be used for you to make appropriate changes.

On the space below make a statement about what you believe your state of wellness is at present.

Visualize yourself in your present state of wellness. In the space below write what you see, hear, and feel, in your mind's eye about the salient features of this picture. Use the lists on pages 41 and 42 to help yourself identify the qualities of your picture.

## WHAT YOU SEE
### (Visual)

brightness

color/black & white

hue or color balance

size

vividness

distance

clarity

location in space

movement

speed

slides/movies

contrast

dimensional/flat

position

associated/dissociated

a.  Are you looking at yourself in the picture?

b.  Are you just out of your own eyes?

c.  Are you a part of the picture?

## WHAT YOU HEAR
### (Auditory)

tone

tempo

volume

location

sound/words

direction

whose voice?

internal/external

timbre

pitch

frequency

distance

## WHAT YOU FEEL
### (Kinesthetic)

temperature

texture

pressure

weight

movement

location in body

moisture

duration

intensity

size

shape

firmness

rough/smooth

Imagine what it would be like five years from now if you did nothing different in your *present state* of health. Pay attention to all the salient features of the picture from now to five years from now, and compare the differences between the present state picture and the future state picture; and write the three main ones below.

1.

2.

3.

IS THIS A FUTURE YOU WANT TO BE REPELLED FROM?

Yes ☐     No ☐

In the space below make a statement about what you want as a *desired state* or optimum wellness. Use the sub-modalities that apply and answer questions a. b., and c about the pictures.

## WHAT YOU SEE
(Visual)

brightness

color/black & white

hue or color balance

size

vividness

distance

clarity

location in space

movement

speed

slides/movies

contrast

dimensional/flat

position

associated/dissociated

a.  Are you looking at yourself in the picture?

b.  Are you just out of your own eyes?

c.  Are you a part of the picture?

## WHAT YOU HEAR
### (Auditory)

tone

tempo

volume

location

sound/words

direction

whose voice?

internal/external

timbre

pitch

frequency

distance

## WHAT YOU FEEL
### (Kinesthetic)

temperature

texture

pressure

weight

movement

location in body

moisture

duration

intensity

size

shape

firmness

rough/smooth

## VISUAL BLENDING

Close your eyes and imagine Jiminey Cricket singing, "Always let your subconscious be your guide." Then hold your hands out separately from both your left and right sides with palms up with your eyes still closed and do the following:

1. Put all the interferences/fears about optimum wellness in a bag and allow it to go in one hand.

2. Allow the healing solution/answers to come into the opposite hand. (You may not consciously know at the moment what that is — but believe that when it comes time to know you'll know). For example: you may not know what you're going to be eating for Sunday dinner two months from now, but when it's appropriate for you to know, you will have that knowledge.)

3. Go through the following for both right and left hands.
   a. Notice the shape, color, size, and any other salient visual features.
   b. Be aware of weight, temperature, firmness, soft/rough and any other salient kinesthetic features.
   c. Listen for any sounds, volume, tempo, thoughts, themes of thoughts and any other salient auditory features.
   c. What is the positive intention of each part? (How is each part helping you?)

4. When you are ready to accept your desired state of optimum wellness then bring both hands together in the center and clasp them very tightly as you integrate and create a new part. (Like the Phoenix which arises anew stronger.)

5. Pay attention to what the new part looks like, feels, sounds, smells, and tastes like.

6. Bring into the new part the following: More brightness and color, sparkle, sound, taste, and smell as you integrate the new part.

# FUTURE TIME

1.  Imagine yourself in the future in 2-3 weeks from now and notice what is different in your old beliefs on present state of optimum wellness. (If you are not getting the results you want add SPARKLE and BRIGHTNESS to your picture and notice what happens.) If you have a positive response move on to number 2; if not, ask your creative self to bring what is needed to have a positive response, and then move on to number 2.

2.  Then imagine yourself in the future in 3-4 months from now and notice what is different in your old beliefs on present state of optimum wellness. Follow the instructions in number 1 if the results are not what you want.

3.  Then imagine yourself in the future 5-6 months from now, and notice what is different in your old beliefs on present state of optimum wellness. Follow the instructions in number 1 if the results are not what you want.

4.  Then imagine yourself in the future in one year from now, and notice what is different in your old beliefs on present state of optimum wellness. Follow the instructions in number 1 if the results are not what you want.

5.  Then imagine yourself in the future in five years from now, and notice what is different in your old beliefs on present state of optimum wellness. Follow the instructions in number 1 if the results are not what you want.

PERSONAL NOTES

# CHAPTER EIGHT

# SELF TALK
## (Affirmations)

As the mind talks, your body listens! Extensive research has shown that your thoughts can raise or lower body temperature, secrete hormones, dilate and constrict arteries, and relax muscles and nerve endings. Biofeedback machines have demonstrated these findings. As a result of this information, it is important that we control the language we use on ourselves. If positive words are expressed, positive results are experienced. The reverse is also true. Winners rarely put themselves down in words before or after a performance. They use techniques called positive feedforward self-talk and positive feedback as part of a training technique, until it becomes a habit.

The inner comments you are constantly making to yourself have been called "mind chatter". These thoughts or self-talk can be controlled. The decision to turn negative thoughts into positive thoughts is yours. One feels more motivated when positive self-talk is used, for there is no opinion as vital to your own well-being and fitness as the one you have of yourself. The Olympic athletes discovered that fitness is as much a state of mind as it is a condition of the body. Directing self talk to desires is critically important to successful achievement. For Example:

I remember, as a child, reading the story of the little engine that believed it could climb a steep hill with an impossible load. It accomplished the task by continually saying to itself, "I think I can" — "I think I can" — "I think I can," then to "I know I can" — "I know I can" — "I know I can," then to "I will" — "I will" — "I will."

Winning athletes utilizing this technique find continued success in meeting personal and team goals. Your mind is like a highly efficient computer. It controls your actions, emotions, and attitudes according to the material it has been given to work with. If you feed your mind negative ideas and information, it can only respond negatively.

If you give it positive, confident material, it will respond in like manner.


# AFFIRMATIONS

An affirmation is the tool that you may use to change your thinking, which in turn changes your attitudes and finally affects your behavior, thereby giving you more choices in life. As you use affirmations with spaced repetition, their impact on attitudes, behavior and feelings becomes a powerful, effective force to change the results of your experience. They are the act of expressing your belief in the truth of a particular statement. Affirmations have been given many names such as self-motivators, self-commands, auto-suggestions or self-talk. They are positive statements about what we believe to be true. Proverbs and sayings learned in childhood are affirmations. For example:

An apple a day keeps the doctor away.
Forewarned is forearmed.
Every cloud has a silver lining.
Smile and the world smiles with you.

The most effective affirmations are those you compose for yourself, based on your own goals, and describes the person you desire to be, the things you want to do or have, and what you want to have or do. As you repeat and write affirmations, you build within yourself the self-confidence, determination, and power you need to overcome obstacles you face in reaching the goals you desire in life.

The power of affirmations may be best demonstrated in this way: Imagine in your mind's eye a balancing scale with a pan on either side. If you are now loaded with negative experiences and attitudes, the negative pan is almost on the ground. Begin to feed positive thoughts and ideas into your mind while the positive side of the scale becomes progressively heavier until it first balances the negative side and takes over and displaces the negative ideas by the sheer force of the weight. The sooner you begin to formulate your own statements to support your personal goals, the sooner you will begin to realize specific benefits from the use of this important tool.

Here are some guidelines for writing your own affirmations:

1. Write affirmations in first person pronoun "I".
2. Write affirmations in the present state.
3. State affirmations positively.
4. Affirmations should be fun and enjoyable.
5. Keep affirmations noncompetitive instead of measuring yourself against others.
6. Affirmations are most effective when tied to an important goal.

Affirmations can help you capture the best of the past, and bring promise into the desired or future, and transform them into the realities of the present. For example:  If you desire to change your eating habits to take off weight, you may write "I enjoy eating fresh fruits and vegetables daily."

## OPTIMUM WELLNESS AFFIRMATION

Prepare one or more affirmation statements in the space below that will assist you in accomplishing the task in this area. Then do the following:  a) Write it on a goal card to carry with you. b) Write it ten times twice daily. c) Say the affirmations to yourself anytime during day or evening.

Imagine two reflections in the mirror of your mind; 1. The person you are today in general wellness.  2) The person you will become in general wellness. Which one are you compelled towards?

Remember, your true potential is in the mirror of your mind. It is your source for the future, and it is the force for today's decisions. Go for wellness!

# PERSONAL NOTES

# CHAPTER NINE

## PHYSICAL DIMENSION

"So, she continued further down the channel in the boat. She floated to a platform to tie up the boat. As she climbed onto it, Pearl discovered a huge green snake. Pearl was so startled and frightened, she screamed. This awakened and alerted the snake of her presence. In her fear she dropped the silver wand in front of the snake, who was now coiled and in an attack position. She was totally immobilized. However, suddenly she remembered that Guidan, the Wizard, had told her one of the gift's that would protect her was her "Golden Magic Cape." She pulled it tightly around her, and the snake relaxed and lost interest in attacking. She had discovered this was truly a cape of invisibility; therefore, she was able to reach down and pick up her silver wand and tap the snake with it. She was immediately freed of his threat and he disintegrated."

Physical wellness begins in many areas of the physical world. The first thing most people are reminded of in this dimension is exercise. Inactivity is a serious health hazard and has been linked to hypertension, chronic fatigue, physiological inefficiency, premature aging, poor and inadequate muscle flexibility. In William Glasser's book on *Positive Addiction,* he says fitness is one certain way to develop characteristics of fulfillment, pleasure, sense of worth and value, and enjoyment of loving and being loved. Donald Ardell in his book, *High Level Wellness* finds that people who take an active interest in keeping fit seem to display a greater abundance of wellness qualities. He went on to include the ability to have more positive interpersonal relationships, fewer risk behaviors, better eating habits, stress management, and greater self-confidence as a result of a consistent, individualized fitness program. In another book by Glasser, *Stations of The Mind,* he discusses exercise increasing the endorphin secretion in the brain which gives a person a greater sense of well being. Some have described the process as "getting high" on your own body's secretions.

Donald Ardell in the book, *High Level Wellness,* lists the following physical fitness principles which have worked for me.

1. Make physical fitness a part of your life. (Decreased disease and illness-prevention advantages of this process.)
2. Look at a fitness program as a lifetime commitment (Important to discover a conditioning activity right for you. Know when you start out appropriately, it always becomes easier, rewarding, and exciting.)
3. Do remember exercising is fun, and don't take an activity too seriously.
4. Supplement exercise routine with well-rounded conditioning. (Routine of stretching and flexibility exercises important.)
5. Learn to distract yourself — and enjoy exercise even more. (Find an outlet wherein you don't have to constantly think about the energy you are expending.)
6. Allow yourself to be in touch with Mother Nature — and yourself. (I have discovered exercise is a great way to commune with environment, with God, and with myself.)
7. Set realistic expectations. (Prevents disappointments and giving up.)

8. You can get better with age. (For those who did not pursue wellness activities in early 20's and 30's the prospects of "getting better" with age through commitment to wellness dimensions are excellent.)

9. Become involved in your program. (Make it an important part of your day; doing so will increase your appreciation and strengthen your commitment.)

10. Learn how to breathe! (Yogis and champion athletes pay close attention to this process and recognize its importance.)

11. Be sensible. (Work into fitness slowly, work with a qualified guide, have a physical-treadmill test, etc.)

12. Consider setting up a contract with yourself to cover at least a three month period, and check off compliance and progress as you go.

Close your eyes and go inside. Imagine Jiminey Cricket singing, "Always let your subconscious be your guide." Then allow to come into your awareness a PICTURE THAT BEST REPRESENTS TO YOU PHYSICAL WELLNESS. Open your eyes, draw the picture below with colored pencils using whatever colors are appropriate for you.

Looking at a continuum from well to dis-ease — 0 being the least physically fit and 10 being optimum physical wellness, circle the number that best represents your state of physical wellness right now.

0    1    2    3    4    5    6    7    8    9    10

Write a statement about what you desire for yourself in the area of physical wellness.

## CATHARSIS WRITING

Close your eyes again, imagine Jiminey Cricket singing, "Always let your subconscious be your guide," as well as your eyes, ears, nose, and mouth. Write PHYSICAL WELLNESS at the top of the next sheet in the workbook. Set a timer for 5 minutes. Then begin writing everything that comes to your mind as quickly as possibly about your concept, experiences, goals, and fears concerning physical wellness. Do not stop until the timer rings. (If you have difficulty writing the full five minutes, repeat the last sentence you wrote until a new thought comes into your mind.)

Close your eyes for a moment, let your subconscious be your guide and say to yourself: PHYSICAL WELLNESS IS:

Open your eyes and write the first ten words that come to your awareness on this page.

1.

2.

3.

4.

5.

6.

7.

8.

9.

10.

Now connect your words in the order you first wrote them to form a sentence or paragraph that makes sense to you. You may add words or change the form of the words you initially wrote to make the connections flow. When you have completed this exercise, you will have discovered what physical wellness means to you at this time. Thank yourself for the important information.

Again close your eyes and imagine Jiminey Cricket singing "Always let your subconscious be your guide." Say to yourself: PHYSICAL DIS-EASE IS: Then open your eyes and write the first 10 words that come into your awareness.

1.

2.

3.

4.

5.

6.

7.

8.

9.

10.

Now, connect your words in the order you first wrote them to form a sentence or paragraph that makes sense to you. You may add words or change the form of the words you initially wrote to make the connections flow. Do this fairly quickly. When you have completed this exercise, you will have discovered what physical dis-ease means to you at this time. Thank yourself for this information.

Close your eyes, go inside again, and imagine Jiminey Cricket singing "Always let your subconscious be your guide," again say to yourself "Physical Wellness to me NOW is: . . . Very quickly write all the one or two word phrases that come into your awareness. Then go back to the predicates in each phrase and categorize them under the six categories listed on pages 65 and 66. You may refer back to the list on pages 64 and 65 to check categories to refresh your memory.

**VISUAL**          **AUDITORY**          **KINESTHETIC**

**OLFACTORY / GUSTATORY**               **UNSPECIFIED**

As you look through this information just completed and become more aware of the process and thoughts you are having about your own state of physical health and well-being, complete the following statements:

What do you want in relation to physical wellness?

How will you know when you have physical wellness?

When and where do you want physical wellness?

What does not having physical wellness do for you? How does it assist you?

What will having physical wellness do for you? What would your life change?

What stops you from having physical wellness?

What resource do you now have to help you move towards your physical wellness goal?

What resources do you now need to help you take the first step toward your physical wellness goal?

What would be a demonstration or tangible sign that you have what you want in physical wellness? When would you know when you had achieved physical wellness?

Set a task for yourself in relationship to physical wellness that once it was accomplished you would know you had achieved your goal. Limit the time period to reach this goal to prove to yourself you're serious about your desire for and are in process with physical wellness. Write down the time and expected completion date. You will widen your choices if you pick a task in an area where your predicates indicate imbalance. For example:

If you have learned from the exercises so far, that you experience the world primarily through vision, (your list of vision words on page 65 is long) set a task for yourself that is kinesthetic or auditory.

1. A visual person may want to set up more feeling opportunities, like experiencing massage.
2. A kinesthetic person who wants to lose weight may want to notice other people's presentations, i.e. body types.
3. An auditory person may want to walk and notice the beauty of nature.

**INTERFERENCES/FEAR:** What Stops You From Achieving Physical Wellness?

Take an 8½ by 11 sheet of paper and divide it into four columns sideways and list across as follows:

Interferences/Fear:    Experience Causing It    Intention    Behavior

Close your eyes and go inside, see and hear Jiminey Cricket singing, "Always let your subconscious be your guide," and be aware of your feelings. Then ask yourself, "What stops me from achieving physical wellness?" Open your eyes and begin writing in Column 1 as quickly as possible the interferences or fear that prevents you from success in the physical wellness. For example: I am afraid to exercise.

In Column 2 write the experience you believe causes this fear. (You may get a picture, have a feeling, or hear something in your memory — write it down briefly.) For example: If I have a beautiful body, I may attract other men to me and be tempted to have an affair.

In Column 3 which is labeled Intention, write down what that interference has done for you in a positive way. (Every behavior has a positive intention, though the results experienced are often negative.) For example: Being heavy protects my marriage.

In Column 4 write two or three things you can do instead to replace the interference with new behaviors that satisfy the intention. (When we have choices in life most individuals are freer and have a decrease in internal stress.)

For example: New behaviors are: Get counseling; acknowledge to my mate that my emotional needs aren't being met, change the pictures in my head, change the way I talk to myself about it.

## ANOTHER EXAMPLE

For example: One interference in achieving physical wellness — is avoiding exercise.

Experience causing it: Takes too much time/effort.

Intention: Protection/comfort.

Behaviors:  These are unique to the individual, for what is comfort to one is stress to another.
 a. Make time schedule.
 b. Short periods of time gradually increased.
 c. Do something fun.

When you are ready to be free of interferences/fears:
 a. Tear off part labeled interferences/fears and experience causing it. THROW IT IN THE GARBAGE OR BURN IT.
 b. Save the intention and behavior and clip it to your work-book page.

| Interference Fear | Cause | Intention | New Choice Behavior |
|---|---|---|---|
| threatens balance of lifestyle | too much time to do it | protection | make time schedule<br><br>do something fun |

Tear Here and Discard

Create a picture in your mind of what you believe your state of physical wellness is at present and make a statement about it in the space below.

In the space below write out what you see, hear, feel, taste, and smell in your mind's eye about the qualities of the picture. (Refer to the list on pages 73 and 74.

## WHAT YOU SEE
## (Visual)

brightness

color/black & white

hue or color balance

size

vividness

distance

clarity

location in space

movement

speed

slides/movies

contrast

dimensional/flat

position

associated/dissociated

a.  Are you looking at yourself in the picture?

b.  Are you just out of your own eyes?

c.  Are you a part of the picture?

## WHAT YOU HEAR
(Auditory)

tone

tempo

volume

location

sound/words

direction

whose voice?

internal/external

timbre

pitch

frequency

distance


## WHAT YOU FEEL
(Kinesthetic)

temperature

texture

pressure

weight

movement

location in body

moisture

duration

intensity

size

shape

firmness

rough/smooth

Close your eyes and go inside and imagine your future or desired state of physical wellness.

1.  Notice if you are drawn to that future and repelled away from
    the present state.
2.  Next, imagine having the physical wellness you want in 5-10-15
    years from now, with the skills, activities and relationships you
    want, as well as the knowledge that you did what you needed
    to do to arrive there. Can you notice yourself being compelled
    to that future and repelled from the present state towards the
    desired state of wellness?    Yes ☐    No ☐
3.  Compare the two pictures of present state and desired state, and
    notice what the differences are in the salient features of each
    picture and list the first three in that order in the space provided
    below.

    a.

    b.

    c.

Now as you notice these two pictures, take the first salient feature. Bring the first feature from the desired state into the present
state picture and notice what happens. What happens to your feelings? Repeat this process for features two and three, paying close
attention to your feelings with each process.

If you are still not getting the results you want, add SPARKLE
and BRIGHTNESS to your pictures and notice what happens.

# VISUAL BLENDING

Again close your eyes and go inside and see, hear, and feel Jiminey Cricket singing his favorite "Always let your subconscious be your guide" song. Then hold your hands out separately from both your left and right sides with palms up with your eyes still closed.

1.  Put all the interferences/fears about physical wellness in a bag and allow them to go into one hand.
2.  Allow the healing solution to come into the opposite hand. (You may not consciously know at this moment what that is — but rest assured when it comes time to know you'll know — like you may not know what you're going to have for Sunday dinner two months from now, but when it is appropriate to know you will have that knowledge.)
3.  Go through the following process for right and left hand.
    a.  Notice the shape, color, size, and any other visual qualities.
    b.  Be aware of weight, temperature, firmness, softness/roughness.
    c.  Listen for any sounds, what thoughts are you thinking, what is volume, tone, tempo, consistency, location.
    d.  What is the positive intention of each part. (How is each part helping you.)
4.  When you are ready to accept your desired physical wellness, then bring both hands together in the center, clasp them very tightly as you integrate the new part.
5.  Pay attention to what the new part looks like, feels like and any sounds.
6.  Bring into the new part the following: More color, sparkle, brightness, sound, taste, and smell as you integrate the new part.

## FUTURE TIME

1. Imagine you're in the future 2-3 weeks from now and notice what is different for you. If you like what you are aware of, move to number two below. If you do not like what you experience—ask what the intention of the objection is and discover what the part still needs and ask your creative self to bring into the objection what is needed to have a positive response.

2. Then imagine yourself in the future in 2-3 months and repeat the process above.

3. Then imagine yourself in the future in 5-6 months and repeat the process above.

4. Then imagine yourself in the future one year from now and repeat the process above.

5. Then imagine yourself in the future five years from now and repeat the process above.

## PHYSICAL WELLNESS AFFIRMATION

Prepare one or more affirmation statements in the space below that will assist you in accomplishing the task in this area. Then do the following:  a) Write it on a goal card to carry with you.  b) Write it ten times twice daily.  c) Say the affirmations to yourself anytime during day or evening.

Imagine two reflections in the mirror of your mind; 1. The person you are today in physical wellness.  2) The person you will become in physical wellness. Which one are you compelled towards?

Remember, your true potential is in the mirror of your mind. It is your source for the future, and it is the force for today's decisions. Go for wellness!

# CHAPTER TEN

## MENTAL DIMENSION

"Pearl was now feeling very happy about having overcome two dangerous encounters. As she floated on down the channel, she suddenly reached the end and realized she would now have to walk through a tunnel in the dark. She came upon a wall, and looked up and saw a huge yellow spider weaving a web across her path. She pulled out her silver wand and touched it with the diamond star. She was instantly freed, for the spider and its web disintegrated."

Close your eyes and go inside. Imagine Jiminey Cricket singing, "Always let your subconscious be your guide." Then allow to come into your awareness a PICTURE THAT BEST REPRESENTS TO YOU MENTAL WELLNESS at this time in your life.

Open your eyes and draw the picture with colored pencils using whatever colors are appropriate for you.

"Use Your Brain for a Change," says Richard Bandler, cofounder of NLP and the creative genius who developed the submodality pieces to NLP. Your brain belongs to you. It is yours to develop, to explore, to expand, and to extend the quality of your life, as well as other's lives. It controls every cell in your body. We are told the average person utilizes only five to ten per cent of the brain cells. My desire is for you to begin tapping into the remaining ninety to ninety-five percent. The interpretation of mental wellness (for the purposes of this successbook) is the more cognitive part which deals with intellectual information, or thinking ability. The following are types of thinking to be considered:

1.  Fluent thinking generates quantity and is able to have an easy flow of thought.
2.  Flexible thinking is the ability to take different approaches to a problem with a variety of ideas, as well as being able to shift categories by taking detours when necessary.
3.  Original thinking is being able to think in novel or unique ways by developing clever or unusual responses.
4.  Elaborative thinking is stretching or expanding ideas or embellishing an idea or adding to it.

In order to increase our thinking ability and enhance mental wellness "mental stretches" are valuable. In other words, do some activity or task which is difficult or hasn't been done before. Attention to the neglected areas means greater wellness for the whole. Thought control is making conscious decisions to decrease negative thinking, by refusing to accept thoughts which are destructive to the mind and body. We do have a choice over what we decide to spend energy thinking about. Allowing ourselves to be victimized or pleased by our own thoughts is our own decision. NOW is the time to TAKE CONTROL of your own thinking processes rather than letting them control you.

## CATHARSIS WRITING

Close your eyes again and imagine Jiminey Cricket singing, "Always let your subconscious be your guide," as well as your eyes, ears, nose, and mouth. Write MENTAL WELLNESS at the top of the next page in your successbook. Set a timer for five minutes. Then begin writing everything that comes to your mind as quickly as possible about your concept, experiences, goals, and fears concerning mental wellness. Do not stop until the timer rings. (If you have a little difficulty writing the full five minutes, repeat the last sentence you wrote until a new thought comes into your mind.)

Close your eyes and imagine Jiminey Cricket singing, "Always let your subconscious be your guide," and your eyes, ears, nose, and mouth. Say to yourself: MENTAL WELLNESS IS:

Open your eyes and write the first ten words that comes to your awareness on this page. You may find yourself being reminded of words as you read a word already written.

1.

2.

3.

4.

5.

6.

7.

8.

9.

10.

Mental wellness means something different to each person, and each meaning is valid. Now, connect your words in the order you first wrote them to form a sentence or paragraph that makes sense to you. You may add words or change the form of the words you initially wrote to make the connections flow. When you have completed this exercise, you will have discovered what wellness means to you at this time. Thank yourself for the impressive information.

Again, close your eyes and imagine Jiminey Cricket singing "Always let your subconscious be your guide." Say to yourself, MENTAL DIS-EASE OR MENTAL ILLNESS IS:   Then open your eyes and write the first ten words that come into your awareness.

1.

2.

3.

4.

5.

6.

7.

8.

9.

10.

Connect these words into a sentence or two, or paragraph, using the words in the order listed above. Do this fairly quickly. Again, you have just discovered what mental dis-ease or mental illness means to you at this time. Thank yourself for this information.

## MENTAL WELLNESS MEANS:

Close your eyes and go inside yourself and bring back the image of Jiminey Cricket singing "Always let your subconscious be your guide." Then hear yourself saying, "MENTAL WELLNESS means to me: . . ." Then open your eyes and write in the space provided below as quickly as possible the words or phrase that comes to your mind. Don't hesitate or analyze the information yet; just write the one or two words that describe best for you the answers to the statement.

Then return to the predicates. Categorize the words under the six headings: Visual, Auditory, Kinesthetic, Olfactory, Gustatory, or Unspecified on the following pages.

**VISUAL**          **AUDITORY**          **KINESTHETIC**

## OLFACTORY / GUSTATORY                UNSPECIFIED

As you look at this information just completed and become more aware of the process and the thoughts you are having about your own state of health and well being, answer the statements following.

What do you want in relation to mental wellness?

How will you know when you have mental wellness for you?

When and where do you want mental wellness?

What does not having mental wellness do for you? How does it assist you?

What will having mental wellness do for you? How would your life change?

What stops you from having mental wellness?

What resources do you now have to help you move towards your mental wellness goal?

What resources do you now need to help you take the first step toward your mental wellness goal?

What would be a demonstration or tangible sign that you have what you want in mental wellness? How would you know when you had achieved mental wellness?

Set a task for yourself in relationship to mental wellness that once it was accomplished you would know you have achieved your goal. Limit the time period to reach this goal to prove to yourself you're serious about your desire for and are in process with mental wellness. Write down the time and expected completion date. You will widen your choices if you choose a task in an area where your predicates indicate imbalance. For example:

If you have learned from the exercises so far, that you experience the world primarily through vision, (your list of vision words on page 87 is long) set a task for yourself that is kinesthetic or auditory.

1.  A person operating with more visual predicates might want to go to the beach and be aware of all the different sounds to broaden auditory and kinesthetic awareness.
2.  A kinesthetic person who is experiencing anxiety may want to notice the internal dialogue about anxiety and turn down the sound.
3.  An auditory person may want to notice happy faces, be aware of happy feelings in the body at the same time to open up more visual and kinesthetic awareness.

### INTERFERENCES/FEAR:   What Stops You From Achieving Mental Wellness?

Take an 8½ by 11 sheet of paper and divide it into four columns sideways and list across as follows:

Interferences/Fear:   Experience Causing It   Intention   Behavior

Close your eyes and go inside, see and hear Jiminey Cricket singing "Always let your subconscious be your guide," and be aware of your feelings. Then ask yourself, "What stops me from achieving mental wellness?" Open your eyes and begin writing in Column 1 as quickly as possible the interferences or fear that prevents you from success in the mental wellness.

In Column 2 write the experience you believe causes this fear. You may get a picture of a memory, have a feeling, or hear something being said by yourself or others when you do this. Write it down briefly.

In Column 3 which is labeled Intention write what that interference has done for you in a positive way. (Every behavior has a positive intention, though the results we experience are often negative.)

In Column 4 write two or three things you can do to replace the interference with new behaviors that satisfy the intention. (When we have choices in life, most individuals are freer and have a decrease in internal stress.)

For example: New behaviors are: Get counseling; acknowledge to my mate that my emotional needs aren't being met, change the pictures in my head, change the way I talk to myself about it.

For example: One of my INTERFERENCES in achieving the mental wellness state I desire might be procrastination.

EXPERIENCE CAUSING IT: My memory of a cause; I remember being forced to do things I didn't want to do and couldn't refuse.

INTENTION: Safety

NEW BEHAVIOR CHOICES: Reward myself as I complete tasks I want to accomplish with:
   a.   Relaxation time with listening to music.
   b.   Watching T.V. comedy.
   c.   Creating a new recipe.
   d.   Swim laps.

(This is unique to each person — for what is helpful for one is stress for another.)

When you are ready to be free of interferences/fears:

1.   Tear off the part labeled interferences/fears — experience causing it and THROW IT IN THE GARBAGE OR BURN IT.
2.   Save the intention and behavior and clip it to your successbook page. Go back to the task set up for yourself as a demonstration of this process, and commit yourself to accomplishing it.

| Interference Fear | Cause | | Intention | New Choice Behavior |
|---|---|---|---|---|
| procrasti- nation | being forced to do things I don't want to do | | safety | relax with music after accomplishing task |

Tear Here and Discard

Create a picture in your mind of what you believe your state of mental wellness is at present and make a statement about it on the space below.

In the space below write what you see, hear, and feel, in your mind's eye about the salient features of the picture. (Refer to the lists on pages 96 and 97.

## WHAT YOU SEE
(Visual)

brightness

color/black & white

hue or color balance

size

vividness

distance

clarity

location in space

movement

speed

slides/movies

contrast

dimensional/flat

position

associated/dissociated

a.  Are you looking at yourself in the picture?

b.  Are you just out of your own eyes?

c.  Are you a part of the picture?

## WHAT YOU HEAR
### (Auditory)

tone

tempo

volume

location

sound/words

direction

whose voice?

internal/external

timbre

pitch

frequency

distance

## WHAT YOU FEEL
### (Kinesthetic)

temperature

texture

pressure

weight

movement

location in body

moisture

duration

intensity

size

shape

firmness

rough/smooth

In the space below make a statement about your goal for mental wellness in the future or in your desired state. Then close your eyes and bring back the image of Jiminey Cricket and see, hear, and feel him singing, "Always let your subconscious be your guide," and open your eyes and write down what you see, hear, feel, taste, and smell about the qualities of that picture.

Imagine what it would be like five years from now if you did nothing different in your present state of health. Pay attention to all the salient features of that present state picture and the one of five years from now, and compare the differences and write the three main ones below.

1.

2.

3.

IS THIS A FUTURE YOU WANT TO BE REPELLED FROM?

Yes ☐      No ☐

## VISUAL BLENDING

Close your eyes and imagine Jiminey Cricket singing, "Always let your subconscious be your guide," Then hold your hands out separately from both your left and right sides with palms up with your eyes still closed.

1.  Put all the interferences/rears about mental wellness in a bag and allow it to go in one hand.
2.  Allow the healing solution/answers to come into the opposite hand. (You may not consciously know at the moment what that is—but believe that when it comes time to know you'll know.) For example: you may not know what you're going to be eating for Sunday dinner two months from now, but when it's appropriate for you to know, you will have that knowledge.)
3.  Go through the following for both right and left hands.
    a.  Notice the shape, color, size, and any other salient visual features.
    b.  Be aware of weight, temperature, firmness, soft/rough and any other salient kinesthetic features.
    c.  Listen for any sounds, volume, tempo, thoughts, themes of thoughts and any other salient auditory features.
    d.  What is the positive intention of each part? (How is each part helping you?)
4.  When you are ready to accept your desired state of emotional wellness, then bring both hands together in the center and clasp them very tightly as you integrate and create a new part. (Like the Phoenix which arises anew stronger.)
5.  Pay attention to what the new part looks like, feels, sounds, smells, and tastes like.
6.  Bring into the new part the following: More brightness and color, sparkle, sound, taste, and smell as you integrate a new part.

## FUTURE TIME

1. Imagine yourself in the future in 2-3 weeks from now and notice what is different in your old beliefs on present state of mental wellness. (If you are not getting the results you want, add SPARKLE and BRIGHTNESS to your picture and notice what happens.) If you have a positive response move on to number 2; if not, ask the creative self to bring what is needed to have a positive response; then move on to number 2.

2. Then imagine yourself in the future in 3-4 months from now and notice what is different in your old beliefs on present state of physical wellness. Follow the instructions in number 1 if the results are not what you want.

3. Then imagine yourself in the future in 5-6 months from now, and notice what is different in your old beliefs on present state of physical wellness. Follow the instructions in number 1 if the results are not what you want.

4. Then imagine yourself in the future in one year from now, and notice what is different in your old beliefs on present state of physical wellness. Follow the instructions in number 1 if the results are not what you want.

5. Then imagine yourself in the future in 5 years from now, and notice what is different in your old beliefs on present state of physical wellness. Follow the instructions in number 1 if the results are not what you want.

## MENTAL WELLNESS AFFIRMATION

Prepare one or more affirmation statements in the space below that will assist you in accomplishing the task in this area. Then do the following:   a) Write it on a goal card to carry with you.  b) Write it ten times twice daily.  c) Say the affirmations to yourself anytime during day or evening.

Imagine two reflections in the mirror of your mind; 1. The person you are today in mental wellness.  2) The person you will become in mental wellness. Which one are you compelled towards?

Remember, your true potential is in the mirror of your mind. It is your source for the future, and it is the force for today's decisions. Go for wellness!

# CHAPTER ELEVEN

# EMOTIONAL DIMENSION

"She returned to the boat and continued softly through the channel. Veering along side the wall, the boat struck it and awakened an alligator. This alligator had a blue glistening skin which had a mesmerizing affect on people and which made its attack easy. But it was startled, and therefore, attacked before Pearl was totally immobilized. Pearl knew her only hope was to touch the alligator with her magic silver wand. Just in the knick of time she raised her silver wand and touched the alligator on the head. It immediately disintegrated!"

Close your eyes and go inside. Imagine Jiminey Cricket singing, "Always let your subconscious be your guide." Then allow to come into your awareness a PICTURE THAT BEST REPRESENTS TO YOU EMOTIONAL WELLNESS at this time in your life.

Open your eyes and draw the picture with colored pencils using whatever colors are appropriate for you.

## EMOTIONAL WELLNESS

The emotional dimension is the affective or feeling domain. The limbic system deep inside the brain is the source of emotions, while thoughts occur in gray matter which is outside the surface of the brain. We respond with both thoughts and feelings to a given situation. The person determines which one to give priority to. Emotions are not good or bad; they just are. Learning to interpret a whole range of emotions from pain, joy, anxiety, jealousy, rage, grief, and fear as an integral part of living, allows an opportunity for you to be fully human and capable of true happiness. A life that is fully lived with feelings is high level wellness. Learning to be aware of what is internal and what is external is one of life's greatest challenges, and results in freely and responsibly expressing emotions. Being unaware of feelings prevents you from breaking old habits. To make the first steps in changing, you need to be aware that an emotion is present.

## CATHARSIS WRITING

Close your eyes again and imagine Jiminey Cricket singing, "Always let your subconscious be your guide," as well as your eyes, ears, nose, and mouth. Write EMOTIONAL WELLNESS at the top of the next page in your successbook. Set a timer for five minutes. Then begin writing everything that comes to your mind as quickly as possible about your concept, experiences, goals, and fears concerning emotional wellness. Do not stop until the timer rings. (If you have a little difficulty writing the full five minutes, repeat the last sentence you wrote until a new thought comes into your mind.)

Close your eyes and imagine Jiminey Cricket singing, "Always let your subconscious be your guide," and your eyes, ears, nose, and mouth. Say to yourself: EMOTIONAL WELLNESS IS:

Open your eyes and write the first ten words that come to your awareness on this page. You may find yourself being reminded of words as you read a word already written.

1.

2.

3.

4.

5.

6.

7.

8.

9.

10.

Emotional wellness means something different to each person, and each meaning is valid. Now, connect your words in the order you first wrote them to form a sentence or paragraph that makes sense to you. You may add words or change the form of the words you initially wrote to make the connections flow. When you have completed this exercise, you will have discovered what wellness means to you at this time. Thank yourself for the impressive information.

Again, close your eyes and imagine Jiminey Cricket singing "Always let your subconscious be your guide." Say to yourself: EMOTIONAL DIS-EASE OR ILLNESS IS: . . . then open your eyes and write the first ten words that come into your awareness.

1.

2.

3.

4.

5.

6.

7.

8.

9.

10.

Connect these words into a sentence or two, or paragraph, using the words in the order listed above. Do this fairly quickly. Again, you have just discovered what emotional dis-ease or emotional illness means to you at this time. Thank yourself for this information.

## EMOTIONAL WELLNESS MEANS:

Close your eyes and go inside yourself and bring back the image of Jiminey Cricket singing, "Always let your subconscious be your guide." Then hear yourself saying, "EMOTIONAL WELLNESS means to me: . . ." Then open your eyes and write in the space provided below as quickly as possible the words or phrase that comes to your mind. Don't hesitate or analyze the information yet; just write the one or two words that describe best for you the answers to the statement.

Then return to the predicates and categorize the words under the six headings:  Visual, Auditory, Kinesthetic, Olfactory/Gustatory, or Unspecified on the following pages.

**VISUAL**          **AUDITORY**          **KINESTHETIC**

## OLFACTORY / GUSTATORY

## UNSPECIFIED

As you look at this information just completed and become more aware of the process and the thoughts you are having about your own state of health and well being, answer the statements following.

What do you want in relation to emotional wellness?

How will you know when you have emotional wellness for you?

When and where do you want emotional wellness?

What does not having emotional wellness do for you? How does it assist you?

What will having emotional wellness do for you? How would your life change?

What stops you from having emotional wellness?

What resources do you now have to help you move towards your emotional wellness goal?

What resources do you now need to help you take the first step toward your emotional wellness goal?

What would be a demonstration or tangible sign that you have what you want in emotional wellness? How would you know when you had achieved emotional wellness?

Set a task for yourself in relationship to emotional wellness that once it was accomplished you would know you have achieved your goal. Limit the time period to reach this goal to prove to yourself you're serious about your desire for and are in process with emotional wellness. Write down the time and expected completion date. You will widen your choices if you choose a task in an area where your predicates indicate an imbalance. For example:

If you have learned from the exercises so far, that you experience the world primarily through vision, set a task for yourself that is kinesthetic or auditory. (Check your lists on pages 111 and 112.)

1.   A visual person (who has a bad temper) might want to beat a cushion in a safe room.
2.   A kinesthetic person might call a friend and talk over a situation to broaden auditory awareness.
3.   An auditory person may run until anger is gone to broaden kinesthetic awareness.

### INTERFERENCES/FEAR   What Stops You From Achieving Emotional Wellness?

Take an 8½ by 11 sheet of paper and divide it into four columns sideways and list across as follows:

Interferences/Fear:   Experience Causing It   Intention   Behavior

Close your eyes and go inside, see and hear Jiminey Cricket singing "Always let your subconscious be your guide," and be aware of your feelings. Then ask yourself "What stops me from achieving emotional wellness?" Open your eyes and begin writing in Column 1 as quickly as possible the interference or fear that prevents you from the success in emotional wellness you want.

In Column 2 write the experience you believe causes this fear. You may get a picture of a memory, have a feeling, or hear something being said by yourself or others when you do this. Write it down briefly.

In Column 3 which is labeled Intention write down what that interference has done for you in a positive way. (Every behavior has a positive intention though the results experienced are often negative.) For example: being heavy protects my marriage.

In Column 4 write two or three things you can do to replace the interference with new behaviors that satisfy the intention. (When we have choices in life, most individuals are freer and have a decrease in internal stress.)

For example: New behaviors are: Get counseling; acknowledge to my mate that my emotional needs aren't being met, change the pictures in my head, change the way I talk to myself about it.

For example: One of my INTERFERENCES in achieving the emotional wellness state I desire might be a volitile temper.

EXPERIENCE CAUSING IT: My memory of a cause; I remember watching my father's explosive temper.

INTENTION:  Independence

NEW BEHAVIOR CHOICES:   Reward myself as I handle anger productively by:
   a. Count to 10 before speaking.
   b. Deliberately lower voice.
   c. Move to another room.
   d. Write down anger
   e. Beat a pillow first.
(This is unique to each person — for what is helpful for one is stress for another.)

When you are ready to be free of interferences/fears:

1.   Tear off the part labeled interferences/fears — experience causing it and THROW IT IN THE GARBAGE OR BURN IT.
2.   Save the intention and behavior and clip it to your successbook page. Go back to the task set up for yourself as a demonstration of this process, and commit yourself to accomplishing it.

| Interference Fear | Cause | Intention | New Choice Behavior |
|---|---|---|---|
| volitile temper | watching Father explode | independence | count to ten before speaking |

Tear Here and Discard

Create a picture in your mind of what you believe your state of emotional wellness is at present and make a statement about it in the space below.

In the space below write what you see, hear, and feel, in your mind's eye about the salient features of the picture. (Refer to lists on pages 120 and 121.)

## WHAT YOU SEE
## (Visual)

brightness

color/black & white

hue or color balance

size

vividness

distance

clarity

location in space

movement

speed

slides/movies

contrast

dimensional/flat

position

associated/dissociated

a.  Are you looking at yourself in the picture?

b.  Are you just out of your own eyes?

c.  Are you a part of the picture?

## WHAT YOU HEAR
### (Auditory)

tone

tempo

volume

location

sound/words

direction

whose voice?

internal/external

timbre

pitch

frequency

distance


## WHAT YOU FEEL
### (Kinesthetic)

temperature

texture

pressure

weight

movement

location in body

moisture

duration

intensity

size

shape

firmness

rough/smooth

In the space below make a statement about what you want as a future or desired state of emotional wellness. Then close your eyes and bring back the image of Jiminey Cricket and see, hear, and feel him singing, "Always let your subconscious be your guide," and open your eyes and write down what you see, hear, feel, taste and smell about the qualities of the picture the statement evokes.

Imagine what it would be like five years from now if you did nothing different in your present state of health. Pay attention to all the salient features of that present state picture and the one of five years from now, and compare the differences and write the three main ones below:

1.

2.

3.

IS THIS A FUTURE YOU WANT TO BE REPELLED FROM?

Yes ☐      No ☐

## VISUAL BLENDING

Close your eyes and imagine Jiminey Cricket singing, "Always let your subconscious be your guide." Then hold your hands out separately from both your left and right sides with palms up with your eyes still closed.

1. Put all the interferences/fears about emotional wellness in a bag and allow it to go in one hand.
2. Allow the healing solution/answers to come into the opposite hand. (You may not consciously know at the moment what that is—but believe that when it comes time to know you'll know.) For example: you may not know what you're going to be eating for Sunday dinner two months from now, but when it's appropriate for you to know, you will have that knowledge.)
3. Go through the following for both right and left hands.
   a. Notice the shape, color, size, and any other salient visual features.
   b. Be aware of weight, temperature, firmness, soft/rough and any other salient kinesthetic features.
   c. Listen for any sounds, volume, tempo, thoughts, themes of thoughts and any other salient auditory features.
   d. What is the positive intention of each part. (How is each part helping you?)
4. When you are ready to accept your desired state of social wellness, then bring both hands together in the center and clasp them very tightly as you integrate and create a new part. (Like the Phoenix which arises anew stronger.)
5. Pay attention to what the new part looks like, feels, sounds, smells, and tastes like.
6. Bring into the new part the following: More brightness and color, sparkle, sound, taste, and smell as you integrate a new part.

# FUTURE TIME

1.  Imagine yourself in the future in 2-3 weeks from now and notice what is different in your old beliefs on present state of emotional wellness. (If you are not getting the results you want add SPARKLE and BRIGHTNESS to your picture and notice what happens.) If you have a positive response, move on to number 2; if not, ask the creative self to bring what is needed to have a positive response; then move on to number 2.

2.  Then imagine yourself in the future in 3-4 months from now and notice what is different in your old beliefs on present state of emotional wellness. Follow the instructions in number 1 if the results are not what you want.

3.  Then imagine yourself in the future 5-6 months from now, and notice what is different in your old beliefs on present state of emotional wellness. Follow the instructions in number 1 if the results are not what you want.

4.  Then imagine yourself in the future in one year from now, and notice what is different in your old beliefs on present state of emotional wellness. Follow the instructions in number 1 if the results are not what you want.

5.  Then imagine yourself in the future in 5 years from now, and notice what is different in your old beliefs on present state of emotional wellness. Follow the instructions in number 1 if the results are not what you want.

## EMOTIONAL WELLNESS AFFIRMATION

Prepare one or more affirmation statements in the space below that will assist you in accomplishing the task in this area. Then do the following:   a) Write it on a goal card to carry with you.   b) Write it ten times twice daily.   c) Say the affirmations to yourself anytime during day or evening.

Imagine two reflections in the mirror of your mind; 1. The person you are today in emotional wellness. 2) The person you will become in emotional wellness. Which one are you compelled towards?

Remember, your true potential is in the mirror of your mind. It is your source for the future, and it is the force for today's decisions. Go for wellness!

# CHAPTER TWELVE

## SOCIAL DIMENSION

"She walked for what seemed like hours. In some parts of the tunnel she had to crawl on her hands and knees. There seemed only to be enough light to see a short distance. Then she arrived in a larger area with a high wall, and crouched in a corner sleeping was a large orange tiger. Fortunately, she saw him before he awakened. When he saw her, he made one ferocious growl and leaped toward her. This time she was ready with the "Golden Cape" wrapped around her and easily touched the center of his head with the diamond star from the silver Wand. The tiger disintegrated as easily as the others."

Close your eyes and go inside. Imagine Jiminey Cricket singing, "Always let your subconscious be your guide." Then allow to come into your awareness a PICTURE THAT BEST REPRESENTS TO YOU SOCIAL WELLNESS at this time in your life. Open your eyes and draw the picture with colored pencils using whatever colors are appropriate for you.

## SOCIAL WELLNESS

Human beings are gregarious by nature. The desire to be around others of likeness is innate. Social WELLNESS includes multiple factors involving relationships both internal and external. Our self-concept develops through socialization. Our self-concept consists of ideas, feelings, values, and beliefs about ourselves, since all our social interactions create the perception we have of ourselves. Self perception, families, school, job, and activities are areas of social concern. How these interact together in a person's environment are of the utmost importance to total balance. These interactions are unique to each individual and culture. As you discover in a new way what it means to have social wellness, the curiosity created by this new learning process will continue to sprout and grow appropriately.

## CATHARSIS WRITING

Close your eyes again and imagine Jiminey Cricket singing, "Always let your subconscious be your guide," as well as your eyes, ears, nose, and mouth. Write SOCIAL WELLNESS at the top of the next page in your successbook. Set a timer for five minutes. Then begin writing everything that comes to your mind as quickly as possible about your concept, experiences, goals, and fears concerning social wellness. Do not stop until the timer rings. (If you have a little difficulty writing the full five minutes, repeat the last sentence you wrote until a new thought comes into your mind.)

Close your eyes and imagine Jiminey Cricket singing, "Always let your subconscious be your guide," and your eyes, ears, nose, and mouth. Say to yourself SOCIAL WELLNESS IS:

Open your eyes and write the first ten words that comes to your awareness on this page. You may find yourself being reminded of words as you read a word already written.

1.

2.

3.

4.

5.

6.

7.

8.

9.

10.

Social wellness means something different to each person, and each meaning is valid. Now, connect your words in the order you first wrote them to form a sentence or paragraph that makes sense to you. You may add words or change the form of the words you initially wrote to make the connections flow. When you have completed this exercise, you will have discovered what wellness means to you at this time. Thank yourself for the impressive information.

Again, close your eyes and imagine Jiminey Cricket singing "Always let your subconscious be your guide." Say to yourself: SOCIAL DIS-EASE OR ILLNESS IS . . . then open your eyes and write the first ten words that come into your awareness.

1.

2.

3.

4.

5.

6.

7.

8.

9.

10.

Connect these words into a sentence or two, or paragraph, using the words in the order listed above. Do this fairly quickly. Again, you have just discovered what social dis-ease or social illness means to you at this time. Thank yourself for this information.

## SOCIAL WELLNESS MEANS:

Close your eyes and go inside yourself and bring back the image of Jiminey Cricket singing, "Always let your subconscious be your guide." Then hear yourself saying, "SOCIAL WELLNESS means to me: . . . " Then open your eyes and write in the space provided below as quickly as possible the words or phrase that comes to your mind. Don't hesitate or analyze the information yet; just write the one or two words that describe best for you the answers to the statement.

**VISUAL**          **AUDITORY**          **KINESTHETIC**

**OLFACTORY / GUSTATORY**          **UNSPECIFIED**

As you look at this information just completed and become more aware of the process and the thoughts you are having about your own state of health and well being, answer the statements following.

What do you want in relation to social wellness?

How will you know when you have social wellness for you?

When and where do you want social wellness?

What does not having social wellness do for you? How does it assist you?

What will having social wellness do for you? How would your life change?

What stops you from having social wellness?

What resources do you now have to help you move towards your social wellness goal?

What resources do you now need to help you take the first step toward your social wellness goal?

What would be a demonstration or tangible sign that you have what you want in social wellness? How would you know when you had achieved social wellness?

Set a task for yourself in relationship to social wellness that once it was accomplished you would know you have achieved your goal. Limit the time period to reach this goal to prove to yourself you're serious about your desire for and are in process with social wellness. Write down the time and expected completion date. You will widen your choices if you choose a task in an area where your predicates indicate imbalance. For example:

If you have learned from the exercises so far, that you experience the world primarily through vision, (your list of vision words on page 135 is long) set a task for yourself that is kinesthetic or auditory.

1. A shy visual person might want to shake a stranger's hand to broaden kinesthetic awareness.
2. A shy kinesthetic person may want to look at faces and smile.
3. A shy auditory person can say "hello" to first five people at work.

## INTERFERENCES/FEAR What Stops You From Achieving Social Wellness?

Take an 8½ by 11 sheet of paper and divide it into four columns sideways and list across as follows:

Interferences/Fear:    Experience Causing It    Intention    Behavior

Close your eyes and go inside, see and hear Jiminey Cricket singing, "Always let your subconscious be your guide," and be aware of your feelings. Then ask yourself, "What stops me from achieving social wellness?" Open your eyes and begin writing in Column 1 as quickly as possible the interferences or fear that prevents you from success in the social wellness you want.

In Column 2 write the experience you believe causes this fear. You may get a picture of a memory, have a feeling, or hear something being said by yourself or others when you do this. Write it down briefly.

In Column 3 which is labeled Intention write what that interference has done for you in a positive way. (Every behavior has a positive intention, though the results we experience are often negative.)

In Column 4 write two or three things you can do to replace the interference with new behaviors that satisfy the intention. (When we have choices in life, most individuals are freer and have a decrease in internal stress.)

For example: New behaviors are: Get counseling, acknowledge to my mate that my emotional needs aren't being met, change the pictures in my head, change the way I talk to myself about it.

For example:   One of my INTERFERENCES in achieving the social wellness state I desire might be shyness.

EXPERIENCE CAUSING IT:   Growing up with dominant parents.

INTENTION:   Protection

NEW BEHAVIOR CHOICES:   Reward myself as I complete tasks I want to accomplish with:
- a.  Say "hello" to stranger on bus.
- b.  Call someone and acknowledge them.
- c.  Thank sales clerk for good service.
- d.  Smile at first 5 people you see in morning.

(This is unique to each person — for what is helpful for one is stress for another.)

When you are ready to be free of interferences/fears:

1.  Tear off the part labeled interferences/fears — experience causing it and THROW IT IN THE GARBAGE OR BURN IT.
2.  Save the intention and behavior and clip it to your workbook page. Go back to the task set up for yourself as a demonstration of this process, and commit yourself to accomplishing it.

| Interference Fear | Cause | Intention | New Choice Behavior |
|---|---|---|---|
| shyness | dominant parents | protection | say "hello" to stranger on bus |

Tear Here and Discard

Create a picture in your mind of what you believe your state of social wellness is at present and make a statement about it on the space below.

In the space below write out what you see, hear, feel, taste, and smell in your mind's eye about the qualities of the picture. (Refer to the lists on pages 144 and 145.

## WHAT YOU SEE
## (Visual)

brightness

color/black & white

hue or color balance

size

vividness

distance

clarity

location in space

movement

speed

slides/movies

contrast

dimensional/flat

position

associated/dissociated

a.  Are you looking at yourself in the picture?

b.  Are you just out of your own eyes?

c.  Are you a part of the picture?

## WHAT YOU HEAR
## (Auditory)

tone

tempo

volume

location

sound/words

direction

whose voice?

internal/external

timbre

pitch

frequency

distance


## WHAT YOU FEEL
## (Kinesthetic)

temperature

texture

pressure

weight

movement

location in body

moisture

duration

intensity

size

shape

firmness

rough/smooth

In the space below make a statement about what you want as a future desired state of social wellness. Then close your eyes and bring back the image of Jiminey Cricket and see, hear, and feel him singing, "Always let your subconscious be your guide," and open your eyes and write down what you see, hear, feel, taste and smell about the qualities of the picture the statement evokes.

Imagine what it would be like five years from now if you did nothing different in your present state of health. Pay attention to all the salient features of that present state picture and the one of five years from now, and compare the differences and write the three main ones below:

1.

2.

3.

## IS THIS A FUTURE YOU WANT TO BE REPELLED FROM?

Yes ☐      No ☐

# VISUAL BLENDING

Close your eyes and imagine Jiminey Cricket singing, "Always let your subconscious be your guide." Then hold your hands out separately from both your left and right sides with palms up with your eyes still closed.

1. Put all the interferences/fears about social wellness in a bag and allow it to go in one hand.
2. Allow the healing solution/answers to come into the opposite hand. (You may not consciously know at the moment what that is—but believe that when it comes time to know you'll know.) For example: you may not know what you're going to be eating for Sunday dinner two months from now, but when it's appropriate for you to know you will have that knowledge.)
3. Go through the following for both right and left hands.
   a. Notice the shape, color, size, and any other salient visual features.
   b. Be aware of weight, temperature, firmness, soft/rough and any other salient kinesthetic features.
   c. Listen for any sounds, volume, tempo, thoughts, themes of thoughts and any other salient auditory features.
   d. What is the positive intention of each part. (How is each part helping you?)
4. When you are ready to accept your desired state of mental wellness, then bring both hands together in the center and clasp them very tightly as you integrate and create a new part. (Like the Phoenix which arises anew stronger.)
5. Pay attention to what the new part looks like, feels, sounds, smells, and tastes like.
6. Bring into the new part the following: More brightness and color, sparkle, sound, taste, and smell as you integrate a new part.

## FUTURE TIME

1.  Imagine yourself in the future in 2-3 weeks from now and notice what is different in your old beliefs on present state of social wellness. (If you are not getting the results you want add SPARKLE and BRIGHTNESS to your picture and notice what happens.) If you have a positive response, move on to number 2; if not ask the creative self to bring what is needed to have a positive response; then move on to number 2.

2.  Then imagine yourself in the future in 3-4 months from now and notice what is different in your old beliefs on present state of social wellness. Follow the instructions in number 1 if the results are not what you want.

3.  Then imagine yourself in the future 5-6 months from now, and notice what is different in your old beliefs on present state of social wellness. Follow the instructions in number 1 if the results are not what you want.

4.  Then imagine yourself in the future in one year from now, and notice what is different in your old beliefs on present state of social wellness. Follow the instructions in number 1 if the results are not what you want.

5.  Then imagine yourself in the future in 5 years from now, and notice what is different in your old beliefs on present state of social wellness. Follow the instructions in number 1 if the results are not what you want.

## SOCIAL WELLNESS AFFIRMATION

Prepare one or more affirmation statements in the space below that will assist you in accomplishing the task in this area. Then do the following:   a) Write it on a goal card to carry with you. b) Write it ten times twice daily. c) Say the affirmations to yourself anytime during day or evening.

Imagine two reflections in the mirror of your mind; 1. The person you are today in social wellness. 2) The person you will become in social wellness. Which one are you compelled towards?

Remember, your true potential is in the mirror of your mind. It is your source for the future, and it is the force for today's decisions. Go for wellness!

# CHAPTER THIRTEEN

## SPIRITUAL DIMENSION

"With each battle she overcame, her internal strength and confidence grew. At the end of the tunnel, Pearl came upon another large body of water and there on the edge waiting was Guidan, the Wizard. She was so happy to see him! He told her this was the last and most treacherous part of the journey. She would have to climb onto a raft to cross the water to the other side of the cave because there was no bridge. He told her to be very careful and have the silver wand ready because a crafty, evil being, called Gruell that was part man and part fish lived in the water. She climbed onto the raft and prepared to cross the narrow waterway. Suddendly, the water rippled, and the nasty, evil looking Gruell appeared. He swam very close to the raft, but she was prepared, and touched his body with the diamond star. A huge burst of purple light filled the entire area and Gruell disintegrated, and what swam off in its place was a beautiful white fish that said, "Thank you Princess for freeing me. I will be eternally grateful.""

## SPIRITUAL WELLNESS

Close your eyes and go inside. Imagine Jiminey Cricket singing, "Always let your subconscious be your guide," Then allow to come into your awareness a PICTURE THAT BEST REPRESENTS TO YOU SPIRITUAL WELLNESS at this time in your life.

Open your eyes and draw the picture with colored pencils using whatever colors are appropriate for you.

Spirituality is awareness of oneself in harmony with the universe. The experience of being at one with a higher power outside of ourselves is uplifting and exciting. Almost everyone has been moved to tears by a beautiful sunset, a piece of music or art, the ocean, breathtaking mountains or an overwhelming love for another person. At these moments the loneliness or narcissistic self-containment dissolves for a while and the impact of truly being connected to something or someone outside ourselves is experienced. At the same time we become deeply connected to ourselves. The issue here is that there is no one way for a person to reach spiritual awareness. One thing we can be sure of is that when spirituality is integrated into our daily living, it makes even the best of lives more meaningful. The ability to let go of judgments and negative destructive thinking brings more peace to our inner soul. One of the amazing characteristics of spiritual wellness is intensified self-valuing, mental clarity, and the development of a forgiving nature. Life can take on a new purpose and the limiting boundaries of the physical, mental, emotional and social dimensions disappear. Unconditional love is truly a living meditation that can dissolve old patterns, while inspiring new physical, emotional, mental and social balance which leads to optimum well-being.

The following poem by an unknown author has this history. A gentleman from New York was sojourning in June 1885 at a Christian home for tourists in Edinburg, Scotland. A copy of this poem was presented to him by its proprietor, and during many lonely hours — which occur even in the most pleasant of foreign journeys — it was often read, and always with great comfort. On the traveler's return, he had a few copies of it printed for free distribution. The demand was so large that a recent edition of 60,000 has been issued.

There is a mystery in human hearts,
And though we be encircled by a host,
Of those who love us well and are beloved,
To every one of us, from time to time,
There comes a sense of utter loneliness.
Our dearest friend is "stranger" to our joy,
And cannot realize our bitterness.
"There is not one who really understands,
Not one to enter into all I feel;"

Such is the cry of each of us in turn.
We wander in a "solitary way."
No matter what or where our lot may be;
Each heart, mysterious even to itself,
Must live its inner life in solitude.

And would you know the reason why this is?
It is because the Lord desires our love.
In every heart he wishes to be first.
He therefore keeps the secret-key Himself,
To open all its chambers, and to bless
With perfect sympathy and holy peace
Each solitary soul which comes to him.
So when we feel this loneliness, it is
The voice of Jesus saying, "Come to me."
And every time we are "Not understood,"
It is a call to us to come again;
For GOD alone can satisfy the soul,
And those who walk with Him from day to day,
Can never have a "solitary way."

And when beneath some heavy cross you faint,
And say, "I cannot bear this load alone."
You say the truth. God made it purposely
So heavy that you must return to Him.
The bitter grief which "no one understands"
Conveys a secret message from the Kind,
Entreating you to come to Him again,
The Man of Sorrows understands it well,
In all points tempted He can feel with you,
You cannot come too often, or too near.
The Son of God is infinite in grace.
His presence satisfies the longing soul,
And those who walk with Him from day to day
Can never have "A SOLITARY WAY."

## CATHARSIS WRITING

Close your eyes again and imagine Jiminey Cricket singing, "Always let your subconscious be your guide," as well as your eyes, ears, nose, and mouth. Write SPIRITUAL WELLNESS at the top of the next page in your successbook. Set a timer for five minutes. Then begin writing everything that comes to your mind as quickly as possible about your concept, experiences, goals, and fears concerning spiritual wellness. Do not stop until the timer rings. (If you have a little difficulty writing the full five minutes, repeat the last sentence you wrote until a new thought comes into your mind.)

Close your eyes and imagine Jiminey Cricket singing, "Always let your subconscious be your guide," and your eyes, ears, nose, and mouth. Say to yourself: SPIRITUAL WELLNESS IS...

Open your eyes and write the first ten words that come to your awareness on this page. You may find yourself being reminded of words as you read a word already written.

1.

2.

3.

4.

5.

6.

7.

8.

9.

10.

Spiritual wellness means something different to each person, and each meaning is valid. Now, connect your words in the order you first wrote them to form a sentence or paragraph that makes sense to you. You may add words or change the form of the words you initially wrote to make the connections flow. When you have completed this exercise, you will have discovered what wellness means to you at this time. Thank yourself for the impressive information.

Again, close your eyes and imagine Jiminey Cricket singing "Always let your subconscious be your guide." Say to yourself: SPIRI-
TUAL DIS-EASE OR ILLNESS IS . . .  then open your eyes and
write the first ten words that come into your awareness.

1.

2.

3.

4.

5.

6.

7.

8.

9.

10.

Connect these words into a sentence or two, or paragraph, using the words in the order listed above. Do this fairly quickly. Again, you have just discovered what spiritual dis-ease or spiritual illness means to you at this time. Thank yourself for this information.

## SPIRITUAL WELLNESS MEANS:

Close your eyes and go inside yourself and bring back the image of Jiminey Cricket singing, "Always let your subconscious be your guide." Then hear yourself saying, "SPIRITUAL WELLNESS means to me: . . ." Then open your eyes and write in the space provided below as quickly as possible the words or phrase that comes to your mind. Don't hesitate or analyze the information yet; just write the one or two words that describe best for you the answers to the statement.

Then return to the predicates, categorize the words under the six headings: Visual, Auditory, Kinesthetic, Olfactory/Gustatory, or Unspecified on the following page.

**VISUAL**          **AUDITORY**          **KINESTHETIC**

**OLFACTORY / GUSTATORY**                    **UNSPECIFIED**

As you look at this information just completed and become more aware of the process and the thoughts you are having about your own state of health and well being, answer the statements following.

What do you want in relation to spiritual wellness?

How will you know when you have spiritual wellness for you?

When and where do you want spiritual wellness?

What does not having spiritual wellness do for you? How does it assist you?

What will having spiritual wellness do for you? How would your life change?

What stops you from having spiritual wellness?

What resources do you now have to help you move towards your spiritual wellness goal?

What resources do you now need to help you take the first step toward your spiritual wellness goal?

What would be a demonstration or tangible sign that you have what you want in spiritual wellness? How would you know when you had achieved spiritual wellness?

Set a task for yourself in relationship to spiritual wellness that once it was accomplished you would know your have achieved your goal. Limit the time period to reach this goal to prove to yourself you're serious about your desire for and are in process with spiritual wellness. Write down the time and expected completion date. You will widen your choices if you pick a task in an area where your predicates indicate imbalance. For example:

If you have learned from the exercises so far, that you experience the world primarily through vision, (your list of vision words on page 160 is long) set a task for yourself that is kinesthetic or auditory.

1.  A visual person might want to go to the mountain and experience nature.
2.  A kinesthetic person might go to a concert and focus on the sounds.
3.  An auditory person may want to go to a funny or sad movie and focus on feelings.

## INTERFERENCES/FEAR    What Stops You From Achieving Spiritual Wellness?

Take an 8½ by 11 sheet of paper and divide it into four columns sideways and list across as follows:

Interferences/Fear:    Experience Causing It    Intention    Behavior

Close your eyes and go inside, see and hear Jiminey Cricket singing, "Always let your subconscious be your guide," and be aware of your feelings. Then ask yourself, "What stops me from achieving spiritual wellness?" Open your eyes and begin writing in Column 1 as quickly as possible the interferences or fear that prevents you from the success in spiritual wellness you want.

In Column 2 write the experience you believe causes this fear. You may get a picture of a memory, have a feeling, or hear something being said by yourself or others when you do this. Write it down briefly.

In Column 3 which is labeled Intention write what that interference has done for you in a positive way. (Every behavior has a positive intention, though the results we experience are often negative.)

In Column 4 write two or three things you can do to replace the interference with new behaviors that satisfy the intention. (When we have choices in life, most individuals are freer and have a decrease in internal stress.)

For example: New behaviors are: Get counseling, acknowledge to my mate that my emotional needs aren't being met, change the pictures in my head, change the way I talk to myself about it.

For example:  One of my INTERFERENCES in achieving the spiritual wellness state I desire might be fear of being left alone.

EXPERIENCE CAUSING IT:  My memory of my sibling's death and feeling lonely.

INTENTION:  Protection and safety

NEW BEHAVIOR CHOICES:
   a.  Enjoy walking on the beach alone.
   b.  Meditation 20 minutes twice a day.
   c.  Going for a hike alone in mountains and experiencing an appreciation of God in nature.
   d.  Running.

(This is unique to each person — for what is helpful for one is stress for another.)

When you are ready to be free of interferences/fears:

1.  Tear off the part labeled interferences/fears — experience causing it and THROW IT IN THE GARBAGE OR BURN IT.
2.  Save the intention and behavior and clip it to your successbook page. Go back to the task set up for yourself as a demonstration of this process, and commit yourself to accomplishing it.

| Interference Fear | Cause | Intention | New Choice Behavior |
|---|---|---|---|
| fear of being alone | sibling's death | safety | enjoy walk on beach alone |

Tear Here and Discard

Create a picture in your mind of what you believe your state of spiritual wellness is at present and make a statement about it in the space below.

In the space below write what you see, hear, and feel, in your mind's eye about the salient features of the picture. (Refer to the lists on pages 169 and 170.)

As you imagine the desired state in your mind's eye, write down what you see, hear and feel about the qualities or salient features of the picture as listed below:

## WHAT YOU SEE
### (Visual)

brightness

color/black & white

hue or color balance

size

vividness

distance

clarity

location in space

movement

speed

slides/movies

contrast

dimensional/flat

position

associated/dissociated

a.  Are you looking at yourself in the picture?

b.  Are you just out of your own eyes?

c.  Are you a part of the picture?

## WHAT YOU HEAR
### (Auditory)

tone

tempo

volume

location

sound/words

direction

whose voice?

internal/external

timbre

pitch

frequency

distance

## WHAT YOU FEEL
### (Kinesthetic)

temperature

texture

pressure

weight

movement

location in body

moisture

duration

intensity

size

shape

firmness

rough/smooth

In the space below make a statement about what you declare as a future or desired state of spiritual wellness. Then close your eyes and bring back the image of Jiminey Cricket and see, hear, and feel him singing, "Always let your subconscious be your guide," and open your eyes and write down what you see, hear, feel, taste and smell about the qualities of the picture the statement evokes.

Imagine what it would be like five years from now if you did nothing different in your present state of health. Pay attention to all the salient features of that present state picture and the one of five years from now, and compare the differences and write the three main ones below:

1.

2.

3.

IS THIS A FUTURE YOU WANT TO BE REPELLED FROM?

Yes ☐      No ☐

## VISUAL BLENDING

Close your eyes and imagine Jiminey Cricket singing, "Always let your subconscious be your guide." Then hold your hands out separately from both your left and right sides with palms up with your eyes still closed.

1. Put all the interferences/fears about spiritual wellness in a bag and allow it to go in one hand.
2. Allow the healing solution/answers to come into the opposite hand. (You may not consciously know at the moment what that is—but believe that when it comes time to know you'll know.) For example: you may not know what you're going to be eating for Sunday dinner two months from now, but when it's appropriate for you to know you will have that knowledge.)
3. Go through the following for both right and left hands.
   a. Notice the shape, color, size, and any other salient visual features.
   b. Be aware of weight, temperature, firmness, soft/rough and any other salient kinesthetic features.
   c. Listen for any sounds, volume, tempo, thoughts, themes of thoughts and any other salient auditory features.
   d. What is the positive intention of each part. (How is each part helping you?)
4. When you are ready to accept your desired state of spiritual wellness, then bring both hands together in the center and clasp them very tightly as you integrate and create a new part. (Like the Phoenix which arises anew stronger.)
5. Pay attention to what the new part looks like, feels, sounds, smells, and tastes like.
6. Bring into the new part the following: More brightness and color, sparkle, sound, taste, and smell as you integrate a new part.

# FUTURE TIME

1.  Imagine yourself in the future in 2-3 weeks from now and notice what is different in your old beliefs on present state of spiritual wellness. (If you are not getting the results you want add SPARKLE and BRIGHTNESS to your picture and notice what happens.) If you have a positive response, move on to number 2; if not ask the creative self to bring what is needed to have a positive response, then move on to number 2.

2.  Then imagine yourself in the future in 3-4 months from now and notice what is different in your old beliefs on present state of spiritual wellness. Follow the instructions in number 1 if the results are not what you want.

3.  Then imagine yourself in the future 5-6 months from now, and notice what is different in your old beliefs on present state of spiritual wellness. Follow the instructions in number 1 if the results are not what you want.

4.  Then imagine yourself in the future in one year from now, and notice what is different in your old beliefs on present state of spiritual wellness. Follow the instructions in number 1 if the results are not what you want.

5.  Then imagine yourself in the future in 5 years from now, and notice what is different in your old beliefs on present state of spiritual wellness. Follow the instructions in number 1 if the results are not what you want.

## SPIRITUAL WELLNESS AFFIRMATION

Prepare one or more affirmation statements in the space below that will assist you in accomplishing the task in this area. Then do the following:   a) Write it on a goal card to carry with you.  b) Write it ten times twice daily.  c) Say the affirmations to yourself anytime during day or evening.

Imagine two reflections in the mirror of your mind; 1. The person you are today in spiritual wellness.  2) The person you will become in spiritual wellness. Which one are you compelled towards?

Remember, your true potential is in the mirror of your mind. It is your source for the future, and it is the force for today's decisions. Go for wellness!

PERSONAL NOTES

## CLOSING

"Princess Pearl arrived across the water to the farthest end of the cave, to complete the last lap of the journey. A freer and happier feeling arose within her than she'd ever experienced before . . . . before . . . . . . . . . .

The people recognized Princess Pearl at once, even though she was tattered, torn, dirty, and bleeding. The Princess's father and mother (King and Queen), came out to greet her, embraced her and welcomed her home. Her parents said, "We thought you were lost and would never be found. We are so happy you have returned."

Much joy and happiness radiated throughout the Village as their Princess told of her travels and particularly of her last, most perilous journey. As a result of this whole experience, Princess Pearl was able to bring news to the Magic Village about the Dark Place and how she had been able to return to the Channel of Life with the help of Guidan the Wizard. Everyone noticed the confidence and maturity the Princess now exuded. Not only did she possess loveliness and compassion, but her outer beauty was matched by the inner beauty and inner strength that no one could take from her. So, this was a wonderful, beautiful day, in which Princess Pearl married her Handsome Prince. And she lived a very long, happy, creative and fruitful life."

PERSONAL NOTES

# EPILOGUE

"No man is an island, entire of itself:
every man is a piece of the Continent, a part
of the maine . . . Any man's death diminishes me,
because I am involved in Mankinde; and therefore
Never send to know for whom the bell tolls: It tolls
for thee."

'Devotions' by John Donne

In summary I want to reiterate the idea that as human beings, we are not only physical bodies, but intellectual, emotional, social, and spiritual entities, as well. This concept is being recognized and affirmed in the new era of holistic medicine. It is only as we come into balance and harmony with these parts of ourselves and accept natural emotion that we will become truly whole and healthy. This is both our challenge and our birthright.

Eilliot Goldwag, in his book *Inner Balance*, has this to say, "The disease-oriented model that has dominated our high cost of national health care system has outlived its usefulness. It needs to be modified. The emerging wave of thought about holistic health reminds us of this need. The "whole" person is physical, mental, and spiritual being; and unless that person is functioning in balance and harmony, the frequent end product is illness. The consciousness of holistic health promises to be the area which the greatest advances in total health care will be seen . . . . The common denominator in achieving success is always to strive toward the recognition of the need for a greater spiritual awareness among all the people. Such growth is the central core in the maintenance of individual health and happiness. (p. 329)

I believe the model represented in this book supports the holistic approach to life. The process demonstrated can take as long or short a time as you decide. This is your life and you are creating your own model. It is a continuum of assessing, planning, implementing, and evaluating to get what you want from life. The arrival of the health care of the future depends on the energy and efforts of everyone to reform our system and to rediscover and accept the importance of the whole person. Antonin Artaud, from the book, *The Secret of Life Extension* by John A. Man says:

"The human body dies only because we have forgotten how to transform it and change it."

## FOLLOW YOUR OWN STAR

So, as a pictorial representation of what you had been experiencing through this process, close your eyes again and imagine Jiminey Cricket singing, "Always let your subconscious be your guide." Then in your mind's eye imagine the five pointed star again. Notice how each area needs to be colored. Then open your eyes and draw and color the star to represent balance for you in those areas now.

Relate it to the physical, mental, emotional, social and spiritual dimensions for you at this time. See, feel, and hear yourself with harmony and balance in your life. Notice the fitness, joy, new skills, activities, the exciting relationships, peace of mind, in your life and be aware that you did what was necessary to care for yourself and to be in this spot. Then, imagine yourself on through your life, five, ten, fifteen years from now, being in this spot of caring for yourself and notice how your life is coming from the future you now have. Does this compel you towards balanced wellness? If so, contract with yourself to make that continually happen for you below in a statement.

Imagine the opposite process of not tending to yourself. Notice what happens to your body, mind, emotions, spirituality, and relationships if you do not do what is necessary to keep in balance and harmony in your life. Then imagine five, ten, fifteen years from now, being in the spot of not caring for yourself and even needing someone else to care for you, and how different your life would be from that frame. Is that a goal that you want for your life? If so, make a contract now with yourself to prevent that from happening, by allowing the compelling future to be a reality for you. Make a contractual statement on the space provided below.

## COMPLETION

And so, we come to the end of our journey; I as the writer and you as the reader and participant of this successbook. It has been an important process for me, as it involved living my life in the model. I hope it has been useful for you as well. I would welcome feedback from any who care to give it about your own personal work as you've gone through this process. You may reach me through the publisher. I am available for consultation, conversation, and teaching. In closing I would like to quote M. G. Richards in his book, *Centering*, when he says:

"Illumination grows within us, sometimes like a swift mutation, sometimes like the yellowing aura of spring. But most readily it comes if we give up all that we have in order to be open-souled when it comes. That it may take its shape WHOLE in us." (p. 147)

PERSONAL NOTES

# BIBLIOGRAPHY

Ardell, Donald, HIGH LEVEL WELLNESS, Rodale Press, Emmaus, Pa. 1977.

Bandler, Richard, USING YOUR BRAIN FOR A CHANGE, Moab, Utah, Real People Press, 1985.

Bandler, Richard, and Grinder, John, REFRAMING, Moab, Utah, Real People Press, 1985.

Bandler-Cameron, Leslie; Gordon, David; Lebeau, Michael, KNOW HOW Guided Programs for Investing Your Own Best Future, San Rafael, Calif., Future Pace Inc. 1985.

Beck, Marie Cornelia, R.N.M.S.E.Ph.D; Rawlins, Ruth Parmelee, R.N. M.S.E.; Williams, Sopphronia R., R.M.M.S.N., Mental Health — Psychiatric Nursing (A Realistic Life Care Approach); C.V. Mosby Col, St. Louis, Toronto, Canada 1984.

Brooks, Jane; Boas, Phil. ADVANCED TECHNIQUES IN NLP, Book I; Metamorphous Press, Portland, Oregon 1985.

Dilts, Robert; Grinder, John; Bandler, Richard; Bandler; Leslie; Delozier, Judith; NEURO LINGUISTICS PROGRAMMING Vol. I, THE STUDY OF THE STRUCTURE OF SUBJECTIVE EXPERIENCE, Meta Publications, Cupertino, Calif., Meta Publications, 1980.

Dilts, Robert, APPLICATIONS OF NEURO-LINGUISTIC PRO—GRAMMING, Meta Publications, Cupertino, Calif.

Gaylen, Williard M.D., FEELINGS; Ballantine Books, New York, New York, 1981.

Glasser, Wm., M.D.; STATIONS OF THE MIND; Harper and Rowe, 1981.

Goldway, Elliott M. ed., INNER BALANCE; Prentice-Hall, Inc., Englewood Cliffs, New Jersey, 1979.

Halpern, Joshua and Reuben, LIVE YOUR HEALTH; Ross Books, Berkeley, Calif.

Havens, Ronald A., WISDOM OF ERICKSON; Irvington, Publisher Inc., New York, New York, 1983.

Kostere, Kim; Malatesta, Linda, GET THE RESULTS YOU WANT, A Systematic Approach to NLP; Metamorphous Press, Portland, Oregon 1987.

Lee, Scout; Summers, Jan, THE CHALLENGE OF EXCELLENCE, Vol. I, Learning The Ropes of Change; Metamorphous Press, Portland, Oregon, 1986.

Lee, Scout, THE EXCELLENCE PRINCIPLE, UTILIZING NLP; Metamorphous Press, Portland, Oregon, 1986.

Lewis, Byron; Pucelik, Frank, MAGIC DEMYSTIFIED; Metamorphous Press, Portland, Oregon, 1982.

McMaster, Michael D., PERFORMANCE MANAGEMENT, CREATING THE CONDITIONS FOR RESULTS; Metamorphous Press, Portland, Oregon, 1987.

Mann, John A., THE SECRETS OF LIFE EXTENSION, How to Halt or Reverse The Aging Process and Live A Long and Healthy Life; Harbor Publishing Co., Berkeley, Calif., 1980.

Marvell-Mell, Linnaea, BASIC TECHNIQUES IN NEUROLINGUISTIC PROGRAMMING; Metamorphous Press, Portland, Oregon, 1982.

Osborne, Cecil, THE ART OF BECOMING A WHOLE PERSON; World Books, New York, New York, 1978.

Segal, Jeanne Dr., FEELING GREAT; Unity Press, Santa Cruz, Calif. 1981.

Selye, Hans, STRESS WITHOUT DISTRESS; J. B. Lippincott, Philadelphia, New York, 1979.

Travis, John, M.D.; Ryan, Sara Regina, WELLNESS WORKBOOK, Ten Speed Press, Berkeley, Calif., 1981.

Tubesing, Donald A., WHOLISTIC HEALTH, A Whole-Person Approach to Primary Health Care; Human Sciences Press, New York, New York, 1979.

CAROLYN TAYLOR, Psychiatric and Mental Health
   Nurse Practitioner

As a health care professional, Carolyn Taylor has served as a nurse, as an educator and as a behavior modification therapist. With a master practitioner level in Neuro-Linguistic Programming, Ms. Taylor capably serves the client base of The Taylor Group, her NLP-rooted organization in Portland, Oregon. With certification in advanced submodalities intervention, Carolyn Taylor contributes to the health care community through C.E.A.R.P. accredited seminars conducted on behalf of other health care professionals.

Ms. Taylor received her M.N., P/MHNP from the University of Oregon Health Sciences University in 1976. She is a Certified Specialist with the American Nurses Association and a trainer for New Choices Workshops.